Letters From Languedoc

Howard Burton

First published in 2021 by Open Agenda Publishing Inc.
Copyright © 2021 Howard Burton

Open Agenda Publishing Inc.
7 Mead Court
Toronto, Ontario
M2L 2A5
Canada

All rights reserved.

ISBN: 978-1-77170-139-6 (pb)
ISBN: 978-1-77170-138-9 (ebook)

About The Author

Howard Burton is the author of three other books: *Exceptionally Upsetting: How Americans are increasingly confusing knowledge with opinion & what can be done about it*, *First Principles: Building Perimeter Institute* and *Burning Down UNESCO: A Guide to Innovative Fundraising*.

He holds a PhD in physics, an MA in philosophy, and was the founding executive director of Perimeter Institute for Theoretical Physics from 1999-2007.

In 2012 he founded Ideas Roadshow, which was broadened into Ideas On Film in 2021. He has created dozens of films and edited over 100 books based upon detailed, long-format conversations with internationally renowned experts in a wide variety of different subject areas.

Visit www.ideas-on-film.com for more details on all books and films. He lives in France.

Contents

Preface	10
Taking the Plunge	13
Meeting the Neighbours	23
Settling In	35
On Education	44
Round Pegs & Square Holes	58
Francophilia	71
Going Native (slowly)	84
On The Ground	100
Restlessness	109
A Decision	121
The End of the Affair	130
Postscript	138

To Louis and Emmy

LETTERS FROM LANGUEDOC

Preface

The letters that make up *Letters From Languedoc* are based on (and are in many cases virtually unedited) real letters written to our French friends in Waterloo, Canada in the late summer and early fall of 2007, right after I left my position at Perimeter Institute and our family moved to France.

I had been invited to publish them in serialized form for a Canadian newspaper at the time, but somehow never got around to doing so, occasionally thinking of resuscitating them over the years when I was encouraged to do so by the few people I had shown them to.

And still, I hesitated. There were always lots of other more pressing things to do, and it never seemed the right moment to seriously consider formally publishing lightly-edited correspondence from a distant time and place.

But in March 2021, in the middle of the seemingly unending pandemic we are all grappling with, the situation had changed. I had recently published *Exceptionally Upsetting: How Americans are increasingly confusing knowledge with opinion & what can be done about it*, which, in turn, prompted me to prepare second editions of both my history of Perimeter Institute (*First Principles: Building Perimeter Institute*) and ruminations on my brief, and somewhat bizarre, experience as an intergovernmental fundraiser (*Burning Down UNESCO: A Guide To Innovative Fundraising*).

Examining all three works simultaneously forced me to recognize the many commonalities between them. Ostensibly about three very different topics—building a research institute from scratch, UN fundraising and the current crisis in American sociopolitical life—it became clear that several overlapping themes were tackled throughout all three: the role of government, the societal underappreciation of research and scholarship, the goals of education, societal values, and so on.

I began to wonder if now might be a good time to take another look at *Letters From Languedoc*, which I only dimly remembered, to see if it might make a worthy fit to what had become, suddenly, a body of work.

And so it proved to be. While obviously different in many ways, *Letters From Languedoc* does provide, I think, a number of revealing comparisons of North American and French society (broadly defined) made all the more vivid from the perspective of someone "just off the boat", as it were.

I decided, then, to add it to the others as the last published member of my "social commentary tetralogy"—if only to force me to finally stop at four of these things, you will doubtless be relieved to learn.

One final word: I've elected, as is the case for all of our Ideas Roadshow books, to use Canadian spelling throughout. In addition to the obvious fact that, as a Canadian, this sort of spelling naturally comes easiest to me and "seems right", Canadian spelling has two other highly salient advantages.

1. Given that nobody really knows what the proper rules are for Canadian spelling, there is far more latitude, and the inevitable errors that will intrude have a much better chance of being viewed as a peculiarity of spelling rather than simply the mistakes that they likely are.

2. Canadian spelling has the singular advantage of irritating everyone: Americans will flinch at "neighbour" and "travelling", while the British will shake their heads at "organize" and "tire". Given that a major incentive for embarking upon social commentary is to shake people out of their pre-conceived biases, it's clear to me that Canadian spelling is the ideal choice for the job at hand.

Saint-Genis-les-Ollières, France; March 2021

Taking the Plunge

August 26, 2007

Dear N & L,

And so it begins. After a brief three-day stopover in London (long enough, however, for us to quickly become overwhelmed at the prospect of $10 lattes—and, rather more unexpectedly, for Emmy to pick up a faux-British accent that she is proudly parading around with as we speak)—we are safely ensconced in our sunny Languedocian abode.

Getting here was largely straightforward, notwithstanding the fact that Montpellier airport taxis are generally incapable of transporting a family of four with 8 hefty suitcases. After sundry arrangements and rearrangements of both ourselves and our belongings, however, we were finally ready to drive off. Judging by his reaction, our driver seemed to have at least dimly heard of Le Pouget, but seemed to have no clear idea of where it actually was. Given our steadfast conviction that we had rented a house in a "neighbouring village of Montpellier" this was vaguely disconcerting, but then, perhaps he was new to the area. At any rate, equipped with a map and the explicit directions that P. had supplied us in advance, we were duly prepared for this eventuality, but as I began relaying the instructions I had in front of me, the taxi driver cut me off impatiently, pointing to the in-house navigation system. No need for all of that detail, I was told condescendingly, all that was required was to type in our destination to this *truc* right in front of us and he would be told, exactly, where to go.

"Ah," I mused contently as I tried to extricate my foot from the duffel bag it was buried under, "The French and their famous love of technology." As I might have mentioned to you, the last time I spent any substantial length of time in your fair land was back in 1989, in the dark antediluvian days before the internet and cell phones. Back then, the French were obsessed with their *minitel*, proudly demonstrating how they could buy train tickets from the comfort of their own home just by typing on a keyboard. And here I was 18 years later, immediately confronted with another example of this embrace of the modern. *Plus ça change, plus c'est la même chose*. I folded the directions and placed them on my lap as I gazed out the window at the low-rise apartment buildings that began to surround us on all sides. Suddenly, the dashboard GPS system came alive as a voice boomed forth authoritatively:

Au prochain rond-point, prenez la deuxième sortie à droite.

"Et voilà!" exclaimed our driver proudly. "Ça marche. C'est simple comme bonjour!"

I smiled back encouragingly, dutifully trying to convey the expected amount of respect for this technological accomplishment that relieved him of the tedium of actually knowing where he was going. The voice, you will likely not be surprised to learn, was female.

And so we arrived, some 45 minutes later, after a surprisingly scenic drive where the hardscrabble scenery of the *garrigue* was interspersed with valleys of vineyards. In the distance lay a line of mountains, the sun glinting off the rocks. No "neighbouring village" of Montpellier this, it seemed. We are well and truly in the country, for better or worse. It was not immediately clear which country, in fact—perhaps we crossed the Spanish border at some point.

Our house amply confirms this conclusion. A sizeable *mas-style* farmhouse complete with about a half-acre or so of brown, scrubby land that regular receives animal interlopers of various sorts, particularly the neighbouring chickens and roosters (3!) who seem to take great pleasure in strutting around in what appears to be a characteristically fowlish manner, clucking and crowing with gay abandon. This was, suffice it to say, not entirely expected, and rather reinforces the rural nature of our abode in direct contrast to its hoped-for (and fully expected) "outskirts" attribute. Internet buyer/renter beware.

In a determined effort to sideline our growing sense of disappointment, put a positive spin on things, and enthusiastically embrace our surroundings (largely, but not exclusively, for the sake of the children), I declared that the presence of the roosters would at least relieve us of the necessity of getting alarm clocks, but even this consolation seems, unfortunately, to be untrue. For it must be admitted that we are in the presence of roosters who seem particularly temporally-challenged, spontaneously breaking into raucous crowing at any time of the day and night and generally incapable of distinguishing one hour from the next. Is this, in fact, normal, I wonder? A particular characteristic of the French *coq*, an independence of spirit that is somehow deeply tied to its fundamentally inspirational role in the national psyche (no flag-waving, militaristic *cocoricos* in Angloland, as you well know—indeed, nothing but the infantile and appropriately pejorative "cock-a-doodle-do")? A way of not-so-subtly harassing unwanted visitors? Do let us know if you have any particular light to shine on this issue—some secret knowledge that your fellow countrymen have deliberately kept hidden from unsuspecting tourists.

At any rate, the ambling poultry belongs, it seems, to our next-door neighbours. They stroll constantly into our yard through a hole in the "fence" (the poultry, that is, not the neighbours—we haven't met them yet), whose principal purpose seems to be to serve as a demarcation between their "eating area" (i.e. their property) and their "recreational zone" (i.e. ours).

As if this sudden flowering of animal life wasn't enough, we also, unexpectedly, have inherited a cat, which P. (doubtless not wishing to scare us away from taking the place) somehow neglected to mention. Arrangements, we later discovered, were made to entrust one of the neighbours with the task of feeding her regularly, but given the fact that she actually *lived* here previously, she was, perhaps not unreasonably, rather put off by our initial unwillingness to welcome her into the bosom of our family, thereby allowing her to retain possession of her territory. After several days of constant howling outside the window—not quite as annoying as the roosters, but still distinctly at odds with the much-vaunted peace and quiet that was so desperately envisioned when we were plotting and scheming our *année sabbatique* around our Waterloo breakfast table last June, benumbed by the cascading droning of lawnmowers—we eventually gave in to her unrelenting feline demands and have since even capitulated to the point of buying cat food for her.

We were quickly rewarded for this act of charity by being regularly presented with a cornucopia of emphatically dead wildlife proudly deposited at our doorstep (mice, snakes (snakes!)), together with sundry remains of other once-living members of the animal kingdom, often unrecognizable. Ah, the joys of country living! Perplexingly, pretty well the only thing "our" cat doesn't seem to have an interest in killing is the one life-form that would be heartily welcome—i.e. the aforementioned temporally-challenged roosters. This I simply cannot understand. Perhaps she is both spiteful and smarter than we have given her credit for (arguably not terribly difficult).

Further explorations *à pied* have confirmed that Le Pouget is, in fact, quite an animal-intensive environment. Stray cats of all sizes and varieties abound; and judging by the growling response one gets by walking past almost every home in the village, virtually everyone owns at least one dog. The favourite breed seems to be that of the mindlessly aggressive mangy variety, although whether this is a deliberate choice or simply a pragmatic response to ensure sufficient protection for the owner (in a vicious circle of self-defense *à la* American gun control) is, for now at least, difficult to determine. One thing that is beyond a shadow of a doubt is that the vast majority of dogs one encounters around here could do with a wash. As could, it must be admitted, the entire town.

I am well aware that you often feel that I err on the side of the romantic. I distinctly remember, for example, that when you learned of our intention to head off to the wilds of Languedoc to experience the joys of simple country living *à la française*, your first words were nothing less than the plaintive and immediate "Have you lost your mind?!" quickly followed by "Think of the children!" before concluding with the self-satisfied and sententious, "You won't last a week!"

All of my appeals and justifications for our decision ("We're tired. We need a change. The kids will be fine—it will be a great experience for them. We just need some quiet and time to reflect.") fell on deaf ears. True, you did listen (albeit smirking indulgently) as I described the glowing future that lay before me in our year of living contemplatively in the South of France: chess with the locals on the sun-soaked square, chatting about French politics with the *boulanger*, the odd game of *pétanque* with the village elders. But it was abundantly clear that you thought me downright delusional.

"Look!" I distinctively remember hearing you bellow into my ear as you grabbed me by the shoulders. "This is no bloody Peter Mayle book we're talking about. This is *Languedoc*. ***Off-season!*** You'll be lucky if you come out of there alive."

So. On further reflection, and with the recent added benefit of actually seeing the local environs—albeit briefly—in all of their naked glory, there *does* seem to be something to your concerns. Our medieval village, while unquestionably authentic, is perhaps often a little *too* authentic for our progressive little New World family. Perched atop a hillside to doubtless repel the sundry invaders of the day (Visigoths? Wayward Crusaders? Expansionist Occitans?), the town is certainly captivating in its own way, but the initial charm of treading along the compact, upwardly spiraling roads does tend to rapidly wear off when one considers that packing an entire community into 50 square metres—while doubtless a pivotal structural design for withstanding medieval siege engines, is rather pointless and out of place in the present day when the greatest threat to one's person is developing a repetitive strain injury due to an overindulgence of video games. Meanwhile all of this enforced togetherness has the undeniably undesirable effect of producing a thoroughly dark and gloomy atmosphere throughout the dank and shady streets. This is particularly unfortunate, given the fact that one of the greatest natural features of this part of the world (consistently remarked upon by sensitive travellers for several centuries now) is the quality of the *light*. Living in the south of France and regularly denying oneself access to the wondrous quality of the surrounding light is like finding oneself in the Louvre and spending all the time staring at the parquet floor. Yet the locals here—strangely, worryingly —don't seem to notice.

Our house, at least, is spared this concern, perched as it is on the recently-erected outskirts of the village (Relief! It **is**, indeed, on the outskirts of **something**!) and thereby accessible to copious quantities of the luxurious light. Inside it is quite spacious and marvellously (almost mysteriously) cool, despite no air conditioning.

It is quite a strange business stepping into someone else's home for a year—driving their car, having your children occupying their children's rooms in the house. It gives one a creepy sense of somehow being catapulted directly into their lives during their absence (they are, as I believe we mentioned to you, presently taking a sabbatical in the US). Perhaps it would be different if we had somehow come to know them beforehand, but under the circumstances there is a disturbingly distasteful feeling that one is somehow imposing, thrusting oneself into places that one has no business being in. But what can we do? A trip to the washroom involves staring at pictures of friends and family while evidence of their frequent travels adorn every wall, giving the place a ramshackle, incoherent feel, rather like a cross between a tiny, provincial museum and a garage sale.

The mother, it appears, is constantly travelling to various developing-world locales, given her heavy involvement in a number of international, often religiously-inclined NGOs (Save the Children, Convert the Children, Save God's Children, Children for Jesus, Children for Mohammed, etc.), while P, a garrulous Scandinavian anaesthesiologist who appears to be shockingly well-integrated in the local scene (***Everybody***, it seems, loves P; even after one week here I have several times experienced enthusiastic greetings from toothless *Pougétois* turn to bemused frowns when they realized that I, rather than he, was behind the wheel of his car), presumably practices a form of medicine somewhere around here. Or perhaps he simply distributes tranquilizers to the locals to enable them to make it through another day.

Ironically, he might well be the only person in the entire area whom I would like to meet—partially because his considerable library (which, his patients might be disconcerted to learn, only contains a handful of medical-related books, and those from the 1970's) demonstrates a locally unique predilection for the written word, but also because it is deeply mysterious to me why an obviously educated fellow would elect to settle his family here of his own free will. It is quite disheartening to realize that the one person around here who might be able to provide concrete reinforcement of my freefalling sentiments of French rural life is the very person who is, necessarily, a continent away from the scene. Doubtless he plays chess as well.

Still, while the odd game of chess would be welcome, for the most part I certainly don't find myself suffering for lack of company. While the villagers are, it should be stressed, notably friendly and patient when one meets them in a shop or some other social setting, I am quite content to be quietly alone, if not downright anti-social, and this seems a particularly good place to do precisely that. While it was unquestionably fun and exciting building and running a research institute, it must also be admitted that the past eight years' worth of frenetic activity—charging around the world preoccupied with the Herculean task of recruiting members of the global intellectual elite to Waterloo, Ontario while triumphantly holding forth to all and sundry on the manifold benefits of theoretical physics—has rather worn me out and brought me to the point where I am nothing less than sick to death of the sound of my own voice. The opportunity to bask in the delights of quiet reflection and contemplation suffuses me with unbridled joy; and the prospect of being marooned in the Mediterranean sunshine, surrounded by people who don't know me, largely have no interest in me and, moreover, speak a different language altogether than the one I've been blathering on unhesitatingly in for the past eight years seems most conducive indeed to my task of quietly reinventing myself before striding off towards the future.

So you can sleep well tonight in the comfort that—yes, indeed—the majority of your dire warnings *do* seem to have been well-founded. Yes, the village is pretty well a dump. Yes, there doesn't seem to be, all things considered, a tremendous amount going on here. Yes, we do most definitely find ourselves squarely located in the back of beyond.

On the other hand, it's been a week now and we're still here. So there. How's ***that*** for resilience? True, under the circumstances, we don't really have anywhere else to go, but that should, I feel, in no way significantly diminish from the strength of this accomplishment. We've lasted a week. Surely the hard part's over now?

Optimistically yours,

Howard

Meeting the Neighbours

September 2, 2007

Dear N & L,

Another paper letter! While we are certainly intent on soon rejoining the ranks of the technological mainstream and sending you regular updates by email as soon as that becomes feasible, it must be sadly admitted that we have not yet managed to procure our home internet service, and thus must content ourselves by relying on both the French and Canadian postal services. Hopefully these missives will reach you before our time in France is completed.

We have now finished week two in Le Pouget and are definitely starting to, if not actually settle in to our surroundings, at least become more aware of them. At the beginning of the week, Richard the poultry-owning neighbour stepped through the fence and introduced himself, hand extended, as we were about to head off in the van to explore the surrounding countryside.

"I hope," he declared, with an air of evident concern as he pumped my hand rhythmically, "the roosters aren't making too much noise for you."

It is difficult to know how, precisely, to respond to this. After a few sleepless nights, one is indeed tempted to say:

"Actually, they are an enormous pain. Please destroy them," but it's rather unlikely that such a reply would have any significant effect other than getting our neighbourly relationship off on the rather wrong foot. So instead, we took the typically Canadian way out and emphatically decried:

"Oh no! *Pas de problème!"* which allowed us to exchange sundry pleasantries (where we were from, how long we were staying, the names of family members and so forth) before piling into our van and heading off, comforted in the knowledge that we had at least begun making contact with the locals and were thus well and truly on our way towards genuine integration in the community. Perhaps in the weeks ahead we could build on this burgeoning relationship and gently cajole *Monsieur le Coq* to keep the blasted things on his own bloody terrain instead of allowing them to indulge in their usual habit of crowing (and defecating) on our back porch right underneath our bedroom window.

A few days later, the possibilities for yet further local integration presented themselves as we encountered the neighbours on our other side. Anita and Ger are, as luck would have it, of a decidedly Netherlandish persuasion and immediately took to the fair Irena like an adopted daughter, their palpable relief at having a Dutch neighbour evident as they babbled away in their guttural tongue.

Hollanders, as you are doubtless aware, seem to be making quite an imprint in the South of France these days. As ever-increasing numbers of Dutch retirees make their way out of the damp, overcrowded, largely-submerged land of wind and rain into the warm sunshine of the Midi to spend their Golden Years, they are, we're told, encountering increasing levels of hostility from the locals, although it is unclear whether this is simply a case of jealousy towards the rich foreigners who are jacking up regional property values or something more substantial. After spending some time at Anita and Ger's house, watching my children frolic in their immaculate pool surrounded by a beautifully maintained garden, I found it difficult to suppress the thought that perhaps the regional hostility towards the quietly invading Dutch was not so much related to matters of finance *per se,* but rather more to the fact that their organizational, gardening and housekeeping skills (i.e. cleaning every so often) so overwhelmingly trounced the local standard, thereby effortlessly demonstrating that living in the countryside need not necessarily involve an element of wallowing in filth. It was easy to see how any resolute grape-picking *Pougétois*, flatly unwilling to raise his level of hygiene appreciably beyond that of his distant ancestors (*If it was good enough for them...*) might decidedly take umbrage at being so summarily presented with a such a stark counter-example of living conditions right in his own back yard.

At any rate, suffice it to say that we are grateful for their presence here, although you may be amused to know that our actions during the last week have somehow precipitated more interaction between the two sets of neighbours than had hitherto occurred in the past seven years. And not all of it, is seems, is unequivocally positive.

The difficulties started innocently enough, as so many tragedies do, having been ironically instigated by the aforementioned Dutch gardening proficiency. After an enjoyable afternoon frolicking by Anita and Ger's pool, we were ready to return home. Even though their property was directly adjacent to ours, due to the fact that the hedge separating us is impenetrably thick (i.e. distinctly opposed to the unkempt random arrays generally seen in these parts), we were set to retrace the one kilometre walk around the surrounding circular road to take us back to our front entrance when Anita quickly stepped forth and urged us to go directly into our back yard by cutting across *Monsier le Coq's* lawn instead—something which, she informed us smoothly, she does regularly with the full consent of all and sundry.

We shrugged our shoulders and took her instructions, tramping quietly beside a few stray hens (the other poultry was, of course, *chez nous*). About fifteen metres away, I noticed a heavy set woman sitting on the edge of an above-ground pool. Startled, she turned back to look at us and I waved amiably, continuing resolutely on our way before ducking across into our yard.

A few days later, Anita came to see us, flushed with embarrassment.

"You need to come over to our place for dinner!" she declared.

"We *need* to?" we responded, confused.

"It seems that there was an issue the other day when you cut across the lawn."

"An issue?" we repeated again, dumbly.

"Yes. I'm afraid you really shouldn't have done that. It was too early. I thought you knew them already."

"Too early? We met Richard the other day," I countered, desperately trying to get a grasp of what was going on. "Doesn't that count?"

"Not really," she replied. "Oh, it's all my fault! I never should have told you to go across their lawn without being properly introduced!"

I nodded uncomprehendingly, still trying to fathom what "properly introduced" meant, going over our brief initial exchange with Richard to see if I had inadvertently committed some profound social transgression. Perhaps I should have told him to kill the roosters after all?

"It seems to me that the best thing to do now to clear the air is to have a dinner at our place where we can all get together and put this whole business behind us," she continued nervously. "How's Friday at eight for you?"

"Sounds delightful."

If there was ever a dinner party that called for having a few drinks ahead of time, this was definitely it. Irena and I polished off a bottle of *Côtes du Rhône* well in advance and staggered all—*bien sûr*, the long way around—to Anita and Ger's place to arrive shortly after 8. There is always, of course, the question of when to arrive in a foreign environment when one has no real sense of the local customs. Does 8 *really* mean 8? Probably not. But then, what if it somehow happens to on this particular occasion? After all, this was a family dinner with children at the home of Northern Europeans. Given our rapidly-increasing disastrous reputation, could we really afford one more *faux pas*, waltzing in an hour or so after hungry, offended guests had arrived? No, far better simply to show up closer to the allotted time and wait however long would be necessary. We could always drink more in the interim.

We were, of course, early. Ridiculously early. Anita and Ger gave every appearance of having been sleeping when we rang their door bell. As we chatted with them over the hastily pushed-out apéritifs, determined to cautiously suss out the lay of the surrounding land to avoid any future conflicts, we were somewhat intimidated to discover that the two sets of neighbours had never had any significant contact with each other—indeed, this evening's *soirée* was the very first time since the Dutch couple had moved to France that the others had been invited over for dinner. Such was the magnitude, evidently, of the crisis we had unwittingly plunged everyone into—all rather disconcerting. I helped myself to several additional glasses of wine in a vain hope to dull the upcoming pain.

Richard and Béatrice trouped in about 9:30, their two children in tow. Firm handshakes all around for the men, together with the obligatory cheek-kissing with the women. I shuffled up to Béatrice as contritely as possible, determined to demonstrate maximum sensitivity towards someone who was doubtless still very much in the throes of recovering from the shock of encountering her new neighbours tread, albeit distantly, across her rooster-infested terrain (it is worth adding for clarification that she was hardly indulging in skinny-dipping in her pool at the time, as her capacious personal corpus was duly enveloped by an even more capacious bathing suit).

But it turned out, happily, that any concerns of lingering hostility seemed quite overblown as she beamed back at all of us, freely exchanging pecks on the cheek while mewing appreciative remarks to Anita and Ger about the house.

I quickly took the opportunity to capitalize on the fount of goodwill by formally apologizing for our egregious trespassing error, explaining that we were deeply sorry for causing any offense and should have known better, but she laughed airily and dismissed my avowals with a wave of her hand as if to ridicule the entire idea that she might ever have been the slightest bit concerned by such an obvious triviality.

The wine flowed steadily. In a moment of Seinfeldian oddity (life imitating art through the famed "puffy shirt" episode), Richard somewhat bizarrely declared his deep affection for the billowing white shirt he was wearing that, he claimed, proudly reminded him of the Middle Ages. Both of our children were—somewhat incomprehensibly, given the deeply understandable fact that they were resolutely ignoring contact with anyone else—summarily invited to a birthday party for one of their daughters to be held the following day. In short all was going swimmingly. And then, abruptly, it all came to an end. I started talking about politics.

To Canadian ears, of course, this would be a completely predictable turn of events. It is well-known that in polite company, particularly under potentially-strained circumstances, one should stay well and truly away from the three conversational taboos of politics, religion and sex and stick to "safe" subjects like hockey, the weather and the size of one's SUV. But this was **France**—and things here, I remembered fondly from my long-ago student days, were drastically different. France was the home of the art of conversation, a place where controversial dialogue and the cut and thrust of verbal contact was welcomed and encouraged. Discussing politics was hardly to be avoided here—*au contraire!* It was virtually demanded.

Or so I had thought.

Confirmation of the consistently political French temperament appeared on offer when the conversation began seemingly heading irrevocably in that direction, with Béatrice sadly averring the decline of regional educational standards that had led them to begrudgingly decide to place their children at private schools .Yes, indeed, she lamented, things in France were changing, and hardly in a positive direction.

It was time, I decided, to plunge in and make up for previous social gaffes by illustrating my clear understanding of the social zeitgeist. Not appreciating the finer rules of when to tramp across property lines was one thing, but when it came to matters political I was on much safer ground.

Indeed they seemed to be, I responded quickly. Speaking of which, what did they think of Mr Sarkozy, their new president?

Given their apparent concern at declining educational standards and Sarkozy's ambitious plans for comprehensive reform in virtually every conceivable aspect of the domestic and international agenda, I had naively expected some form of at least partial endorsement.

"Sarkozy?" snorted Richard, his shirt fanning out impressively over the dinner table, "He talks a lot."

And so it was precisely here, you see, that things went south. Given the conversation to date, not to mention my fairly wine-addled state of mind, I had naturally assumed that the concern that was being levied towards Mr Sarkozy was the same one I privately shared—sure, there was much to do, but how was it possible that one man could coherently produce the necessary progress in so many disparate areas simultaneously (ambitious foreign policy, reduction of special privileges for unions, reform of the universities, reform of national educational agenda, greater competition for France's cosseted state-run enterprises, a global environmental leadership position and many, many more)? Surely he must prioritize? Surely he must focus?

And so I responded, loudly and passionately, with any sensible linguistic inhibitions long dulled by my copious intake of wine. Of course, I maintained enthusiastically, Sarkozy was a talker. Certainly, he would not be able to achieve even a fifth of his incredibly ambitious agenda. But what a relief to see such an obviously intelligent, energetic, passionate fellow at the helm of one's country! What a welcome change for the likes of me, after witnessing untold years of professional politicians blathering on about nothing other than their own narrow political self-interests, unable or unwilling to formulate even the simplest possible plan for where the country might go and why, to find myself in a country led by someone determined to implement a progressive agenda unashamedly based on some genuinely explicit affirmation of particular values! Here, I rhapsodized emphatically, was someone who genuinely ***led!*** Here was someone who took a stand!

Total silence.

Irena, ever more sensitive than I am to the reception of my various pontifications, reached under the table and squeezed my leg. "Down Boy!" was the message. Too late.

"More paella?" asked Anita solicitously, swiftly returning from the kitchen like an Angel of Mercy in a desperate effort to prevent the entire evening festivities being reduced to rubble. But there were no more takers.

After a few more minutes of awkward silence, Richard leaned back in his chair, swigged another glassful of wine and pronounced slowly:

"That's exactly the problem. He's filled with all sorts of ideas about how to change France. And we're all terrified that he might actually succeed."

One hears a good deal about the famed "urban/rural" divide these days, as wags of all flavours hold forth on how the greatest division of our age is not that of nations or cultures but rather the difference in *mentalité* between urban and rural dwellers, but until one directly experiences at least a small sense of things in the raw, as it were, it is difficult to get a clear sense of what they are talking about.

But here it was in all of its naked splendour: simply put, these people are completely terrified of, and 100% opposed to, change. Of any sort whatsoever. Don't talk to them about how such and such social program is unaffordable. They don't want to hear about crumbling urban infrastructure or fractional shifts in GDP or international competitiveness or necessary investments in renewable energy. Just don't change a thing. And particularly not in poor Languedoc where virtually the entire regional economy is supported by a collection of French and EU subsidies to ensure that widespread overproduction of low-quality wine can be indefinitely maintained.

All in all it was an interesting learning experience, but like most learning experiences it came with a distinct cost. Our French neighbours, initially of the view that we were simply ignorant foreigners, insensitive to basic notions of privacy, are now convinced that we are nothing less than jack-booted fascists, while our Dutch neighbours are profoundly exasperated at our seemingly perverse determination to antagonize their neighbourhood despite whatever Herculean efforts they might indulge in to the contrary.

Meanwhile our dear, innocent children were doomed to spend the better part of the next afternoon standing around helplessly in the blazing heat to attend a birthday party (suffice it to say that, while it was patently obvious that their presence was not desired, not showing up at this stage would have been little less than a full-blown declaration of war) where they knew nobody and could barely communicate.

Such experiences, I told them resolutely, pushing them out the door with an empathetic shake of my head, were all part of the rich tapestry of life. "At least you have each other," I boomed sententiously, resorting to the *sine qua non* of parental tactics—the judiciously placed non-sequitor.

Louis, quite reasonably, was having none of it:

"But why can't we have each other in our *own* house? Why do we have to hang around at a birthday party for people who don't want us there anyway?!"

"Because it's the polite thing to do," I said firmly, closing the door behind them before quickly retreating to an upstairs bedroom with a book. "And at least somebody in this family has to be polite," I murmured to myself, as I hunkered down to read, out of sight of any hostile neighbourhood eyes.

Confidentially yours,

Howard

Settling In

September 9, 2007

Dear N & L,

Thank you very much for your recent letter, as well as, more generally, your willingness to play along with this decidedly low-tech game of *snail mail*. We are still hopeful that we will be able to make the transition to the 21st century at some point and actually engage in regular email contact, but I must confess that, bureaucratic obstacles being what they seem to be around these parts, it is not entirely clear to me when that might actually occur.

It should be emphasized that we had actually been quite prepared for this. The French bureaucracy is, of course, legendary for its Byzantine intricacies and generally stifling mindlessness; and we were determined to approach the entire experience with the right attitude.

It's simply absurd, we assured ourselves knowingly, to head off to the South of France and expect North American-style efficiency. After all, if easily-accessible phone and internet service was our greatest concern, there would be no point in coming here in the first place. We would certainly not turn into some version of those tedious anglophone expats who are forever bitching about the hideous bureaucracy and lazy work ethic of the French that gravely limits our ability to efficiently soak up the Mediterranean sun, desperately trying to eat our cake and have it too.

And yet there are limits.

Let me be clear: I'm not the slightest bit bothered by the fact that everything closes down for at least two hours over lunch. Quite the contrary, in fact: I find it part and parcel of a most sensible approach to living that seems eminently more reasonable than the constant fixation on shopping and petty consumerism that one is besieged with throughout North America. It's 2:15 and the store owner still hasn't returned to open her shop? *Tant pis!* Walk down to a nearby café, buy a newspaper and read for a half hour or so. Waiting in lines is hardly a crisis for me, particularly now that I'm taking some professional time off and thus under no real pressure to go anywhere anyway. The man behind the post office counter wants to have a lengthy chat with a customer about her grand-daughter? *Charmant.* The *boucher* is temporarily indisposed, immersed in the current horse-racing results? Take your time: I'll read my book. Register our children for school? Fill out some forms? Of course. I'll just take a seat in the shade. Triplicate, you say? No problem.

All of this, and more, was met with perfect equanimity and not a little bit of pride at our stalwart ability to smilingly adapt to local life. But then we met our match: the ***banque***. You might think that opening up a bank account would be a fairly trivial affair. After all, we weren't looking for a loan or anything—just some place to park a small portion of our hard-earned money, complete with minimal interest. P., ever-solicitous and doubtless recognizing from bitter experience the fundamental importance of possessing a local bank account to firmly integrate into French society, had already made the requisite demands at the local branch of the *Crédit Agricole* where he did his banking business, and had passed on to us detailed instructions on what we should bring along to open our very own *compte*: our ID and a copy of the rental contract for the house to testify that we were, indeed, living there. Together with some money, of course. It all seemed pretty straightforward.

The first trip to the Le Pouget branch of the CA was not an unpleasant experience. The lady in the tiny office was perfectly warm and friendly, but unfortunately it appeared that our request exceeded her authority. *Hélas* she informed us sadly, the agent who is responsible for opening new bank accounts at that particular establishment was on holidays and wouldn't be back until mid-September. Perhaps, she suggested, we should think of going up the road to Clermont l'Hérault and opening an account at the CA branch there instead?

This seemed reasonable, if somewhat unnecessarily complicated (Why was there only one person designated with the supreme authority to establish new accounts?). Before we strolled away, however, in a fit of bureaucratic insight, I thought to ask her what paperwork would be needed to open up the account. She called over to her contact in Clermont and, after several moments of intense conversation, relayed to us that it would be necessary to have identification, the rental contract, and several copies of bills addressed to us in France.

Well, I replied patiently, we have the first two but don't unfortunately, have the third yet. "Don't you have a phone bill?" she demanded, suddenly astounded.

"No," I replied smilingly, we just arrived a week ago. In fact, we *did* try to get a phone line ordered, but *France Telecom* wouldn't proceed with the order until we had a French bank account—so here we were.

"Oh," she replied confusedly. "I see."

More phone calls to Clermont, more chatter. Finally she turned back to us and announced that we would have to bring copies of bills addressed to us in our home in Canada to open the account. This was really very odd. What on earth would a bill sent to our Canadian address prove? Presumably, after all, we had lived *somewhere* before coming to France and had paid some bills—I mean, how dodgy did we look? Was that really necessary?

But then, in a sudden flash of insight (years of dealing with sundry government and university officials have, I'm proud to say, given me deep insight into the frightening miasma of the bureaucratic mind) I realized what was going on: the rules called for both identification and copies of bills before opening a bank account, and there was simply no way around that. If bills to a French address were not available, then bills to a non-French address would have to suffice. Simple as that.

The next day we headed off to the branch in Clermont to begin again. This time we received a different story: no, we would not need copies of bills sent to our Canadian address, but our file could only be processed during a separate follow-up appointment in a few days time. In the meantime, we needed an official letter of permission from P. stating that he would permit us to open an account.

I swallowed hard. Clearly, I thought to myself ruefully, I had misunderstood. This simply *had* to be a language issue.

"I don't understand," I said, determined to remain calm. "We have a signed copy of the rental agreement right here."

"Yes, I know," she replied mechanically, "But we need a copy of his passport and signed confirmation from him. Do you have a number where he can be reached?"

"No," I said slowly, still trying to grasp a glimmer of reasonableness in this line of reasoning that might have somehow eluded me. "I have his email address, if you'd like to contact him. He's in Washington. But frankly, I have no idea why you are so determined to do so. We're renting a house from him and we have the rental contract right here. The account is for us, not him."

"Of course," she said breezily. "Well, do what you can. We'll see you on Friday."

By the end of the week, my tolerance was wavering. After eight days of diligent efforts to open a simple bank account, we had nothing to show for the experience, while the prospect of obtaining a phone line or an internet connection could only, under our patently bank-less circumstances, be a distant dream.

Friday's appointment, it must be admitted, began badly.

"Alors..." our determined bureaucrat began, looking through our various identification papers "Do you have a copy of P's passport?"

"No..." I began slowly, rhythmically clenching and unclenching my fist to relieve the mounting stress. "As we said last time..."

"Well, I really need to have that," she announced robotically. "We need some identification."

"He **is**, I understand, a customer *at this very bank*," I said stonily. "That is why, in fact, we chose to come here to open an account. If you want some information on him, you should have it in your files somewhere."

This was, of course, a mistake. When confronted by a knife-wielding lunatic screaming at you to defend yourself from the ten foot dragon behind him, it is generally best practice not to acknowledge the presence of said dragon. Similarly, when dealing with mentally comatose bureaucrats insisting on verifying the identity of an **entirely irrelevant** person, it is strongly inadvisable to enter a discussion on how best to procure such verification.

"Client records are confidential," she replied with a condescending sneer. "I don't have access to them. And without full confirmation from your landlord, we simply can't open an account for you. Of course, if you had some other form of proof that you were living there—a bill from *France Telecom* say..."

And so there was simply no further option: my only available recourse was to lose my temper. Much as I would like you to believe that I did so strictly as part of a deliberate, last-ditch, tactical approach to break free from the suffocating tentacles of bureaucratitis, it must be admitted that the lion's share of my vitriol was honest and heartfelt.

It worked, however. Ten minutes after my tirade, we were the proud owners of a French bank account. Clearly, all of this good humour and positive attitude business can only take one so far. Learning, learning...

So there have been a few bureaucratic issues so far. But as you can see, we are slowly learning the appropriate way to deal with them.

You ask many questions about our local environment (number of bakeries, scenery, hiking possibilities and so forth), which makes me realize that I have not done a terribly good job at accurately giving you a flavour of things here. For it must be recognized that I have a natural predilection for focusing on our sundry encounters with various local people (as you might have noticed) and, to put it somewhat gingerly, that is perhaps not the particular strength of this area. I fear, therefore, that I am giving you a rather skewed, and disproportionately negative view of things that I will henceforth try to rectify.

The scenery is ***most*** impressive—far more so than we had been expecting. With its spectacular combination of mountains, rolling hills, charming hilltop villages (particularly if one is not actually in one of them) and vineyards as far as the eye can see, Languedoc has a rugged and beguiling charm that has already seeped well and truly into our skin.

And it is hot. Very hot. Each day seems to be a carbon copy of the last, with nothing but piercing blue skies and bright, sizzling sunshine. Not surprisingly, we have spent some time rigorously investigating most of the surrounding beaches and have settled down on our favourite spot that we visit with considerable regularity—it's a leisurely 40-minute drive away through rustic villages to just beyond Frontignan.

The entire experience is, to use an expression that we have taken to invoke with startling regularity, *extremely easy on the eyes*. The French, it must be stressed, do beauty very well indeed. Certainly, they are blessed with a tremendous amount (one might even say unfair amount) of geographical advantages—soaring mountains, lush river valleys, spectacular rock formations, imposing chateaux, self-consciously beautiful villages built right into the rock, and so forth.

But perhaps the most striking thing about this place is how so much attention is clearly paid to ensure that the beauty will be preserved: diligently putting all of their big-box stores on the well-defined (i.e. non-sprawling) outskirts of every town so as to protect both the charm and vibrancy of the old (typically at least partially pedestrian-free) centre, lining their side roads with rows of willowing, intertwining plane trees that transform routine journeys to the supermarket into sensual joys of driving through a leafy carapace that is dappled with bright Mediterranean light. In France, God bless them, they take their beauty **seriously**—recognizing its intrinsic importance and insisting on harnessing and incorporating it within everyday life.

Contrast this with the incessant and needless visual offensiveness that one finds throughout North America, where horrifically ugly bright pink and green neon signs saturate one's field of view, screaming their mindless slogans and discount offers as loudly as they can to rise above the surrounding, unrelenting din.

We eat almost every breakfast and dinner outside (it's too hot to eat lunch outside). Sunsets on our back porch have quickly become a beloved ritual with each one as anxiously awaited as the hottest television show: pink-tinged clouds and crimson flares magically glowing over the distant hills. Anticipation of this nightly light show goes a considerable way towards blunting any irritation that the French bureaucracy might be able to throw at us during the day.

So as you can plainly see, there is no need to be worried about us at all. *Nous sommes bien ici.* The scenery is spectacular, the weather is delightful and the bureaucracy is for the most part manageable (only requiring the odd tirade here and there to put things to rights—or at least a sort of manageable status). And with the kids poised to start school next week, doubtless further integration into local life will follow, for better or worse. Perhaps I'll soon find that chess partner after all.

Gamely yours,

Howard

On Education

September 16, 2007

Dear N & L,

Greetings again from the wilds of Le Pouget.

The start of the school year was, unsurprisingly, the predominant feature of the Burton household of late, and it has most definitely proven to be an educational experience for all.

We knew a few things, of course, before we started. We understood that, unfortunately, Emmy and Louis would have to go to separate schools due to the fact that the one year that separates them unfortunately falls precisely in the divide that separates elementary school from middle school in France. We knew that the French school day is exceptionally long compared to its North American counterpart, given that it necessarily involves a 2-hour lunch break, thereby effectively running from 9–5 (Emmy, attending the local school in Le Pouget, would at least be able to come home for lunch. No such luck for Louis). Wednesdays, we were told, would only be half-days for Louis (just mornings) and entirely school-free for Emmy, but she would be forced to make up for this mid-week freedom by attending schools on most Saturday mornings (Louis would not). So far so manageable, if rather different from what we were used to. But then, that's part of the whole experience of going somewhere new, no?

We also understood that there exists some sort of natural divide between "private" and "public" schools, with the private schools typically Catholic and the public schools naturally non-denominational. This one was rather more puzzling to me. Increasing numbers of people we spoke with adamantly maintained that the private schools were vastly superior to the public schools (including, but by no means limited to, the puffy-shirted, anti-Sarkozist Monsieur Le Coq and family), uniformly lamenting the decline in the public school system over the past few decades.

When I expressed apparently reasonable concern, not being Catholic or even religiously inclined, at the prospect of placing my children in a Catholic school, I was immediately informed that such concerns were profoundly irrelevant—private schools had no particular sectarian basis; and, in any event, the rigorously secular aspect of the French state (this being the place where headscarves are banned in schools, we were reminded) would ensure that no religious indoctrination could possibly occur.

The whole thing struck me as deeply mysterious. If Catholic schools could not really be fundamentally different from state schools, I mused, what on earth was the point in having them at all? Both were largely supported by the state, with the private schools typically requiring a minor supplement (of the order of 50–100 Euros per month) that, while hardly negligible, was rather far removed from the spectre of typical "private school" fees that I was used to. It is all, in short, spectacularly odd for us.

At any rate, we swiftly learned upon arrival that any desire to investigate the neighbouring Catholic schools would be pointless, as they had long since reached their quotas and were not taking any more children. The state schools, on the other hand, were naturally obliged to accept any new students who came to the area. So it was that Louis came to be enrolled in a Collège in Gignac some 10 km away, while Emmy was naturally placed in the village school in Le Pouget.

The exterior, at least, of Emmy's local school is just fine. Located squarely in the middle of the town, across from the *Mairie* and the local soccer field, it is hardly an imposing presence and could even be called charming at some level.

Louis' Collège, on the other hand, has all of the warmth and conviviality of a penal colony. In the late afternoon the children emerge, blinking into the sunlight, waving their *carnet de liaison* in front of the noses of the patrolling sentinels as they file through a metal gate (No *carnet*, no escape). Loitering outside the school at any given moment can be found various roving bands of mohawk-toting hoods—smoking, swearing, spitting and occasionally punching each other in the upper torso as a means of ribald entertainment.

Another highly worrying sign is the disturbing ratio of boys to girls in the public school system—something like 2:1 in Emmy's school and more like 4:1 in Louis'. Unless France is mysteriously undergoing a democratic sea-change of Chinese proportions, the only conceivable explanation for this is that the vast majority of the girls (together with, one imagines, the majority of boys of the non-mohawk variety) are firmly ensconced in the private-school system.

My feelings of guilt at thrusting my son into such a hideous environment are somewhat diminished by his untenably optimistic attitude as he bounds out of the van each morning with a cheery "See ya later, Dad!" before penetrating the gloomy exterior. He is a remarkable fellow, my son. Were I in his shoes, there's simply no way on earth I could be convinced to go at all into an environment where I was both an outsider and someone who could barely defend myself linguistically. Indeed, expecting precisely this (understandable) reaction, we had already explicitly told him that given the circumstances he was welcome to opt out: his mother and I were prepared to home-school him and procure a French tutor for him somewhere ("No fair!" shouted Emmy immediately, who would doubtless have withdrawn from school immediately if given the choice). But he was, shockingly, undeterred.

"Thanks", he replied calmly. "But I think I'll give the school a real try. I can always leave later if it's that bad."

It was interesting, if a little humbling, to learn that, in Louis' eyes at least, the prospect of being home-schooled by his parents was a terrifying notch or two below whatever the worst of rural Languedoc might be able to throw at him.

You ask how their years of "French immersion" have prepared them for things here. It is difficult to measure this precisely without some sort of suitable comparison (e.g. spending a year in Italy or Germany where they have had no background whatsoever in the language), but there is nonetheless a strong temptation to simply report "not very well". Their comprehension is weak, their ability to express themselves is quite poor, and their grammar is essentially nonexistent.

It should be emphasized that, back home in their Canadian French-immersion programs that they have attended for four or five years, they were both viewed as successful students. And so, while I can hardly claim to have made a rigorous study of the situation, anecdotal evidence certainly suggests to me that anyone who unthinkingly plonks their children in "French immersion" naturally assuming that the experience will produce fluently bilingual (or even reasonably competent French-speaking) children, has a rather significant shock in store for him/her.

They will be perfectly fine, of course, at the end of the day, and will doubtless swiftly surpass us in relatively short order. Children are notoriously elastic in such situations—we have all witnessed many examples of immigrant children (often from strikingly different cultural environments such as Korea or Sudan) arriving in Canada without a word of English transformed into flawlessly babbling English speakers a scant six months later. But it should also be mentioned that the Canadian school system invariably gives such students considerable additional support to help them attain sufficient mastery of the language—here, it seems, such assistance does not seem to be forthcoming. They simply don't appear to know how to handle children who arrive unequipped with the standard linguistical background—and, one is tempted to conclude, don't appear to care terribly much either. Perhaps it has, quite simply, never happened before.

Anyone who has any experience with this issue will appreciate that successful integration strategies necessarily have to be tailored to the characteristics of the child, a point most strikingly illustrated by our personal experiences, given that our two children appear to be at opposite ends of the language confidence spectrum.

Louis remains, for the most part, somehow blissfully unaware of the fact that he can't actually speak the language at all. He plunges in unhesitatingly, speaking quickly, and often nonsensically, all the while gesticulating furiously to demonstrate his point. He seems to be quite persuaded that any lack of comprehension on the part of his interlocutors is somehow their fault. Emmy, on the other hand, naturally much shyer by nature, is terrified to say a word, uncertain as she naturally is of the precise grammatical construction or most appropriate phrase.

In a desperate attempt to relieve the kids of some of their discomfort, we acted on the recommendations given to us by former sabbatical veterans and forthrightly informed them before school began that "this year doesn't count"—that under the circumstances their marks would likely be considerably worse than what they were used to, but that they shouldn't let that get to them: all that would be required would be to try their hardest and do their best.

This announcement was met with resounding enthusiasm and joy by our children, much to my inner amusement given its fundamentally nonsensical nature. After all, what does it really mean for a year to *count* anyway? (In what real way, one is tempted to ask, did their great grades in a French Immersion system actually *count* for them learning to communicate with French speakers?) Moreover, what more can they do under ***any*** circumstances than simply try their hardest and do their best? Ah, to be in the secure cocoon of an orderly world where things *count* or *don't count*, where punishment and rewards are meted out solemnly and judiciously from on high as part and parcel of some Great Reckoning! I seem to have missed that awestruck stage of childhood development myself—my own youth combined a universal scepticism of adult justifications with personally trying to get away with as much as possible from a very early age. I realize all too well the boundless good fortune that allowed me to bring forth children into this world far better than I deserved, but I still can't help feeling frustrated at times when they accept my sententious statements so uncritically. Of course, they are young yet.

Otherwise, things seem to be oscillitating rather dramatically between vertiginous, inspirational highs and dark periods of despair.

The outstanding physical beauty of this area is simply mesmerizing. We have ambled through the breathtaking village of *St Guilhem-le-Désert* after an afternoon's hiking along a nearby ridge under crystal blue skies; we have gazed down (way, way down) upon the splendour of the spectacular *Cirque de Navacelle* while munching delectable roquefort sandwiches and sipping smooth wine; we have stood, spellbound, on our back porch night after night, gazing at the shimmering silhouettes of the nearby mountains as the sun dips gently behind them, overwhelmed by the majestic beauty of our surroundings and counting our lucky stars at having escaped to such a stunning locale.

On the negative side, however, we have had to endure *The Day of the Endless Roundabouts* where we spent hours mired in Montpellier traffic circles after unsuccessfully trying to accomplish various administrative tasks, including establishing a phone and internet connection (hence, still, this *snail mail* correspondence), but by far the most intense period of despair was *The Day of the Decapitated Bunny*.

It was the day following the first day of school—a Wednesday—and I awoke in a splendid mood, delighted that I had survived the previous day's ordeal, which included not only being bombarded by the justifiably overwrought condition of my offspring, but also (at least allegedly) a joint luncheon with Louis' school Principal (he never showed up, as it happened).

I jauntily jumped into our car to drop off Louis at school before returning home to immerse myself in my regular French grammar autodidact session. I was jolted from my reverie on the merits (not to mention point) of the subjunctive, by a piercing scream from outside the house, where Irena had stumbled upon what appeared to be the recently mutilated remains of a rabbit. Now, you must understand that I am not particularly good at this sort of thing. Perhaps better expressed, I am spectacularly horrible at it. I don't do death terribly well, and am worse still when presented with the combination of death and mutilation.

"There's a dead rabbit outside!" bellowed Irena.

I hunkered down, trying to pretend that I didn't hear. The subjunctive form, suddenly, was vastly more intriguing than I had previously realized. But of course, she couldn't be stopped.

"THERE'S A DEAD BUNNY OUTSIDE!"

"WHAT THE HELL DO YOU WANT ME TO DO ABOUT IT?" I shouted back, desperately looking for my headphones to don. "I didn't kill it!"

Faced with this stalemate, and understandably underwhelmed by my lack of flagrant lack of manly skill at dealing with dead animals in our vicinity, Irena left to go shopping, as previously arranged.

I resolved, with the steadfast determination that has long been my personal trademark, to completely forget about the dead rabbit. After all, it was (allegedly) somewhere in the back yard out of sight; and, moreover, was dead—not terribly much to do on that front, it seemed. Moreover, this being Wednesday, Emmy was home for the day and I could merrily spend the morning playing games with her, thereby avoiding both dead animals and the perils of the subjunctive while simultaneously demonstrating my fatherly sensitivity. All in all a very good plan, it seemed.

But no. A few minutes later, the cat popped up on the window ledge and howled, as is her custom, to be let in. When I went to open up the door for the cat, what should I find unceremoniously plopped on our doormat but the aforementioned **DEAD BUNNY**, most assuredly dead, and most assuredly headless to boot.

Well. I screamed. Emmy, quite unused to seeing her father so flagrantly falling apart, was somewhat taken aback.

"What is it!?" she demanded.

"***THERE'S A DEAD BUNNY ON THE MAT!***" I shrieked, horrified.

"Gross!" she summarily declared, with all the enthusiasm that a nine year old can bring to the word.

"Absolutely!" I concurred.

There was a short pause.

"Don't you think you should do something about it?" she asked me.

"*ME?!*" I screamed. "Why should *I* do something?"

"Because you're the parent."

"Too bad: this isn't in the parent handbook—I'll clean diapers and help with homework and teach you how to hit a baseball, but I don't do decapitated bunnies. And anyway, Mom found it first!"

Clearly I was not in top form on the logic front, but I was feeling rather desperate. The fact that I was acting considerably less mature than my nine year old daughter was vaguely concerning, but not nearly so vexing as having to directly confront what lay immediately behind our back door.

Than there was a knock on the front door. Rapid-response taxidermists, perhaps, who could swiftly remove the offensive detritus? No such luck. It was, in fact, the phone guys, coming to install our new line. True, I had been told that they would come somewhere from 3-5 pm that day and it was now 10:30 am or so, but they were, I was informed, in the neighbourhood and thought they might be able to get it done early.

So in they came to install the phone; and all the while they worked I kept wondering whether I shouldn't just ask them to remove the dead bunny as well. It should also be mentioned at this point that I generally have a problem finding the right tone when dealing with people working in my house. It's not so much the language difficulties (although that does tend to exacerbate the problem), but more that I really don't know what to **say** to these people in any language, and invariably find myself looking like some kind of an emasculated weenie owing to my general lack of ability at supposedly male pursuits (plumbing, electrical stuff, mechanical stuff, etc).

The fact that they would laugh at me when confronted with my obvious lack of toughness didn't particularly concern me, but I was worried that at least one of them might be struck by the revolting aspect of the whole business and I would never get phone service again in the future should I ever need it. So I didn't ask them after all and instead morosely waited for Irena to come back from shopping.

Well, as you might imagine, my lovely wife was none too pleased to discover that the decapitated rabbit remains had mysteriously moved closer to our home, and after another unproductive session of screaming, arm-waving and general protestation ("*I didn't come to this God-forsaken place to deal with dead animals. I'm reading **Spinoza** damn it!*"), it was decided that the aforementioned puffy-shirted neighbour (*Monsier Le Coq*) should be summoned to deal with the dastardly situation while I go fetch my son from his morning scholastic incarceration.

There was, of course, the not unreasonable possibility that *Monsieur Le Coq* would be unwilling to assist his fascist neighbours after our disastrous "make-up dinner", but my sense was that his ill-will was largely directed at me rather than Irena (whom he doubtless felt sorry for, not entirely unreasonably) and he might well construe this as an opportunity to somehow "show me up".

Whatever his motivations, he did apparently manage to de-bunnify our back stoop, so clearly the fellow has his uses, roosters and all. Meanwhile, upon picking up my son for his first Wednesday afternoon break, I was appalled to discover that he had, in fact, had no school that day at all and that he had spent the entire morning stuck in the office twiddling his thumbs while being periodically mocked by higher-grade students who *did* have to be there. Not quite as bad as being confronted by mobile headless rabbits, perhaps, but clearly not the best of all possible mornings nonetheless.

We weren't phoned by the school administrative personnel, suffice it say, due to the rather irritating fact that we hadn't yet had a working line, although why we weren't explicit informed of this rather salient scheduling detail (i.e. "**THERE'S NO SCHOOL FOR 6ÈMES UNTIL THURSDAY**") was highly annoying (presumably the rest of the class was orally informed beforehand, but Louis' anglophonic ear didn't pick it up, and they clearly made no effort to ensure that he was aware of the peculiarities of the schedule).

In a fit of pique brought on by the accumulated frustrations of the morning, I decided that I had had enough of subjecting my family to the idiocies of rural French life and I would god-damned well educate my god-damned children in a god-damned place that had god-damned progressed since the god-damned Norman conquest.

I grabbed a local yellow pages (such is our sorry fate these days) and found two "International Schools" in Montpellier. Throwing our children in the back seat of the van, I angrily informed them that, consumed as we were for their welfare, their mother and I had decided to sacrifice our planned afternoon trip to the beach to instead find proper schooling for them and that they bloody well better not god-damned complain about it.

So off we merrily trekked to Montpellier, where several dozen roundabouts later (often the same ones), we were dismayed to discover that the "International Private Schools" that we had imagined in all their prep-school North-Eastern American splendour, were little more than forlorn shacks not much more physically impressive than our Waterloo garage. Moreover, this being Wednesday afternoon, they were closed. We headed home, hot, tired, hungry and generally despondent, having spent the better part of 4 hours driving around uninspiring Montpellier neighbourhoods, consoling ourselves half-heartedly that we would one day laugh about all of this, but inwardly having a hard time imagining when such a moment might actually occur.

"At least," I announced half-heartedly, we have a phone line now. Which was true enough. But then several days later I discovered that the phone guys didn't actually install an ADSL line after all (without informing me), so it is actually quite incompatible with having any effective internet connection.

Still, at least the next time my kid is stuck for hours on end in the office at his Alcatraz-esque educational institution, he can phone me for help—which is something, I suppose. But sometimes not quite as much as we would like.

Regretfully yours,

Howard

Round Pegs & Square Holes

September 23, 2007

Dear N & L,

Another week has elapsed in the balmy south—another 7 days of subjecting ourselves to the vicissitudes of Languedocian life.

A general comment that has to be inserted here is that life seems to pass exceptionally slowly here. There are doubtless many factors responsible for this—long periods of static weather patterns, still-novel relief from the pernicious distractions of gainful employment, being surrounded on all sides by peasants of a remarkably medieval and generally slow-moving mindset—but the composite portrait that one can safely conclude is that our life here often seems to proceed at a snail's pace. Everything, in short, moves slowly here.

Well, that is not actually correct, *almost* everything: the driving is very much typically, suicidally, French. I have to tell you that I actually find this quite amusing: cars and motorcycles recklessly passing on all sides, careening through roundabouts, screeching their tires. Despite this idiotic determination to needlessly jeopardize their lives (and everyone else's) it often still brings a smile to my lips given that it is so overwhelmingly obvious to me that they have nowhere to go anyway.

I am actually (you might be surprised to learn, given our shared Waterloser experiences) a big-city kind of fellow. I understand the hustle-bustle of the modern world and readily expect, when in Paris, London, New York or the like, to be subjected to throbbing masses of people anxiously honking, swearing and swerving to their destinations. But speeding in Le Pouget? In Gignac? In Clermont l'Hérault? ***What on earth for? WHERE THE HELL ARE YOU GOING? WHAT DOES IT MATTER?*** I mean, really, let's be honest here. Irena, who thankfully does all the shopping, informs me that this same bizarre propensity for reckless speed in the hearts and minds of otherwise intellectually-frozen people occurs at the local supermarket, where passionate charioteers wield their carts with a turbo-charged frenzy that would put Michael Schumacher to shame.

In other news, the celebrated *vendange* is now in full swing in these parts, and everywhere one encounters slowly-ambling flatbed trucks filled to the brim with their wares to be summarily poured into the *cave coopérative* to make the local plonk—which in itself is interesting and (for us, at least) unusual enough.

In a fit of investigative fury, Irena and I dropped by the Le Pouget wine-making environs one morning while the kids were at school. Suffice it to say that the whole experience is nothing less than an overwhelming directive to strictly limit one's oenological consumption to *Appellation Contrôlée* products, as we shockingly witnessed snails, mud, leaves, branches and god knows what else being poured, unceremoniously into the local mix.

It seems that, along with the quality of the grape and all the requisite seasonal tending of the soil and so forth throughout the year, one principal feature that distinguishes higher-quality wine from its barrel-scraping brethren is the fact that the grapes of the former are all picked by hand, thereby ensuring that the fermenting mixture is principally made up of little more than the fruit itself.

Doubtless to the local connoisseur, there is something metaphorically satisfying about (literally) imbibing the surrounding countryside, but, spared as we are of any ecstatic feelings of pride towards the *Pougétois terroir,* we quietly opt for splurging 4€ at the local supermarket to purchase a "higher end" (i.e. presumably mud-free) *Côtes du Rhône* instead. Doubtless this, too, does not particularly endear us to the local citizenry (we make our wine purchases quickly and shamefully, like conducting a drug deal, placing the offending bottles at the bottom of a shopping bag that is immediately covered with other products), and in my darker, more paranoid moments I envision our van being deliberately obliterated by one of the enormous Star Wars-esque mechanical grape-pickers that is currently prowling the countryside.

In your last letter, you expressed a concern that Louis' natural confidence might be somewhat diminished by his unfortunate Collège experiences. While it is true that he has not infrequently been buffeted by the slings and arrows of bullet-headed peasant kids who simply cannot comprehend why anyone born outside of the *Département de l'Hérault* might actually attend school here (a confusion, it must be acknowledged, that we are rapidly beginning to sympathize with), I can assure you that he remains, thankfully, as irrepressible as ever, with an impressively buoyant sense of humour.

Of course, it does help that there is so often something very amusing to laugh at.

At the beginning of the year, for example, we naturally assumed that he would be relieved of having to attend the weekly tranche of four hours of English classes that his other classmates were subjected to. After all, he could already speak English considerably better than the teacher (hardly the greatest of accomplishments, it must be admitted)—and, while it cannot be denied that he would theoretically benefit from a rigorous environment in which he would find himself exposed to a detailed analysis of the subtleties of English grammar, it seemed hard to comprehend how his time could be well-spent listening to British pronunciation tapes and learning the English word for *chien*. Perhaps, we ventured to suggest, he could spend his time during English class getting extra help in French instead?

Given the dynamics of the situation, we didn't have a ready opportunity to make this suggestion ourselves to the appropriate authorities, so we instead conferred the responsibility of doing so to our son at the earliest opportunity.

"Ask your English teacher," I earnestly entreated him, "if it would be all right if you could somehow substitute extra help in French for the English class."

When I picked him up later on that afternoon and reminded him of my request, he immediately broke down into paroxysms of laughter.

"Oh yeah!" he exclaimed, "I asked her, just like you told me. And do you know what she said?!"

I shook my head.

"She told me that it was *impossible*! Because it was my *right* to take English and that under no circumstances would I be denied my rights!"

This talk of rights had by now been the butt of many a family dinner-time conversation. Throughout his entire first week of school (or at least those days that he was actually supposed to be there), he had done nothing more than trek from class to class, listening to each successive teacher drone on about *les droits*: the rights of the teacher, the rights of the principal, the rights of the school, the rights of the parents, the rights of the state, the rights of the school nurse, the rights of the parent-teacher association, the rights of the janitors, the rights of the cantine staff, and so forth.

And now, it appears, we had our first tangible instance of the rights of the student: the obligation to sit through a class of rudimentary, poorly-taught education on one's native tongue while being informed of the inadequacies of one's accent by British voice tapes. The fact that the Fifth Republic was somehow fundamentally predicated upon the necessity of teaching English to Anglophonic North Americans gave me an insight into the untrammeled bureaucratic miasma of this country that even surpassed whatever *France Telecom* might manage to throw at me. Which, as you know, is certainly saying something.

And yet even this inanity would be eclipsed by Emmy's experiences. A few days ago we were informed that Emmy would be seen by the region's inspector for an assessment to see if she was suitably fit for integration into the exacting standards of the Le Pouget *école*. Well, fine, I thought. Good for them if they are going to take the trouble to see if every new kid from outside the French system has the necessary background and skills to be properly absorbed. In many ways it struck me as a bit overdone and typically over-formalized—after all, presumably one could just ask one's teacher to see if the situation could be managed—but at least fairly well-intentioned and not altogether unreasonable.

Imagine my surprise, then—not to mention uncontainable amusement—when we met with the inspector after the test and discovered that he had spent a considerable time testing my daughter on her **English** skills. Her English is satisfactory, he duly informed us, but definitely needs some work. Confronted with this stupefying combination of hubris and ignorance, I grabbed the test and immediately pointed out to the respectable gentleman that several questions on the test were, in fact, wrong (confusing and often inappropriate transliterations of French words and expressions).

Suffice it to say that he waved my objections away with a disdainful gesture, leaving me in the rather perplexing position of not knowing whether to belt him for his presumptuousness or hug him for giving me the largest laugh of my week. At the end, I opted to just laugh in his face, which seemed like the most reasonable option under the circumstances.

Perhaps unsurprisingly, he didn't seem to respond to this terribly well, quite taken aback that his bombastic drivel was actually *questioned* (if not, indeed, ridiculed) by a parent. I get the distinct sense that, all of this *rights* business notwithstanding, there is an overwhelming reliance on authority in these parts that, ironically, naturally tends to cow the various members of the system into submission rather than give them a natural platform to assert themselves.

Once again, it is hard to see from my relatively skewed vantage point if this is a local or national phenomenon, but I have a strong sense that it is more reflective of country living than anything else. After all, from my various forays into Paris over the years I have come away with a very decided sense that Parisians don't take too terribly well to being pushed around by anyone. Here, though, things seem strikingly different. Your kid is having trouble at school? Have him repeat a year. Maybe two. People in these parts seem oddly unperturbed by such a flagrant admission of failure. Of course, if this would, in turn, imply the imposition of a rigorous set of academic standards, it might in some ways be defensible. But I can assure you that it is most definitely not.

You ask about bakeries and other such essential aspects of village life. There are, it appears, two in the town, although it must be admitted that, owing to our strict division of household duties (i.e. Irena does all the work and I do all the complaining), I have yet to go inside either one, although I'm told that the personnel are most friendly and accommodating; and the croissants, certainly, are very good.

There is also a local tabac where Irena regularly purchases *Le Figaro*, thereby encountering the scowling tabac man who is, I'm told, uncharacteristically rude to her on a daily basis. She naturally assumes that this is because of her foreign status, that he is one of the few *Pougétois* who is generally disposed to not being warm and welcoming to all and sundry, but I am convinced that it is related to the publication itself. *Le Figaro*, I distinctly recall from my three-month visit to France as a student all those years ago, is not infrequently considered an "extremely conservative far right daily"—so much so that I was reluctant to even buy it when we first arrived (it was the only one remaining on the shelves).

Imagine my surprise, then, when I opened it up to discover that it contained thoughtful balanced commentary and interesting, provocative views. There is also, too, the undeniable fact that they have the strategic marketing sense to be currently offering free Woody Allen DVDs with purchase of the weekend edition. While I have long been, as you know, a fan of Woody Allen, our present circumstances make this offer seem nothing less than a gift from the gods.

While it is always enjoyable to discover a well-written and informative publication, it is vaguely disconcerting that according to the local standard I seem to be mired irretrievably in the extreme *droite* of the political spectrum somewhere to the right of Mussolini—a location where, suffice it to say, I have never felt any previous association. Your thoughts on this? Are you devoted followers of *Libération*? Is our friendship now over?

I am trying, still, to keep some form of an open mind about the locals here, but I must confess it is getting harder and harder to do. Feeling vaguely uncomfortable about the decidedly unimpressive state of my French oral skills, I am torn between a desire to immerse myself in conversations with whomever I might encounter to ameliorate the situation and a fervent wish to retreat to the safe confines of my adopted study where I can merrily wallow undisturbed to contemplate the urgent issues of Early Enlightenment Europe. Invariably, the 17th century wins—not only because of the intrinsically interesting subject matter, but also, it must be admitted, because of my flagrant lack of enthusiasm for any conversation with the locals here, who strike me as cerebrally challenged as any rough-hewn, opinionated type regularly encountered in any small-town Ontario Tim Hortons. There is, not to put too fine a point on it, simply not a great deal to say.

It also doesn't help, I should admit, that I can barely understand them on the few occasions when I am actually interested in doing so. When one's auditory experiences are limited to the crystal clear enunciations of the *France Culture* morning show and the evening news, the prospect of deciphering rural mumblings seems a formidable challenge that is well and truly beyond my current levels of ability and motivation.

As previously mentioned, it should be emphasized that they are, in their own way, quite friendly. Of course one has to know the rules of the game, however. When I first arrived here, determined to make a good impression, I waved cheerfully at every passing person I saw, in unconscious imitation of the behavioural patterns of small-town Canada (or at least what I've seen about them on TV).

Unfortunately, however, this doesn't seem to be done here. Men greet each other warmly, grasping each other resolutely by the shoulders and shaking hands as firmly as is humanly possible as if one has just encountered one's long-lost brother. For an outsider, on the other hand, a simple, subtle head nod in their direction might be appropriate. Meanwhile, the notion of a strange man waving at women (even hunched-over, cane-strutting grandmas as I have been guilty of, in my determination to exhibit an egalitarian spirit) is strictly *interdit* and doubtless considered highly offensive.

Embarrassing stuff, and sadly all too typical. For it must be admitted that we are not integrating terribly well with our fellow Pougétois. In short: we don't fit here terribly well, and I don't think that this has much to do, at the end of the day, with anything at all related to language issues, and everything to do with the fact that we are simply not country people and the French country—at least around here—is, well, *really* country: no exhausted Parisians looking for a way out of the daily grind, no dreamy writers searching for solitude in the hills, no upwardly-mobile paysans desperate to escape and make it in the big city (i.e. Montpellier, say).

No, none of that—at least not so far as we can see. The principal activities in these parts seem to be chatting with one's neighbours and fellow shop-owners, playing *pétanque* (*bien sûr!*) at the local *jeu de boules terrain* (every evening at 5 pm sharp, once the temperature has cooled down), and, more generally, hanging out in doorways and on steps.

There is a café here, of sorts, but suffice it to say that given my relatively slender build, ostentatious lack of tattoos and general unwillingness to indulge in strong alcoholic beverages before 8 am, I don't feel particularly qualified (or motivated) to enter. There are, needless to say, no bookstores here.

There has been, unquestionably, the odd moment of rural charm. The other day, for example, Irena took Louis to the doctor (he needed, *bien sûr,* a *certificat médical* to enable him to participate in school sporting activities where bands of roving thugs can more effectively gang up on him) and was bemused to find herself discussing the difficulties of procuring home internet service in Le Pouget for three quarters of an hour with the very friendly local physician while hacking Pougétois cooled their heels in an over-crowded waiting room. On reflection, I'm not sure that this is a good thing or a bad thing, but it is, most definitely, different.

Still, as time progresses, I am becoming less and less tolerant of the charms of rural living. The wandering chickens and roosters, never much admired, have at this point become quite close to insufferable, and I now find myself inexorably drawn to the hose to spray water at them whenever they come into our yard (which, ironically, has the pleasurable short-term effect of sending them scurrying back to puffy-shirt land, but the distressing longer-term effect of watering the hitherto brown earth that results in more growing seedlings to attract them back at the next possible opportunity).

The cat, meanwhile, continues to spend its waking hours killing surrounding wildlife, of which there is no apparent shortage despite its best efforts, and proudly dropping it on our doorstep.

Our house—N. has repeatedly inquired anxiously about the house, and we have tried to be, in turn: positive, optimistic, tranquil, taciturn, but there is little to be gained in avoiding reality, I'm afraid—is rather a dump, with all the structural soundness—and, rather more alarmingly, hygienic standards—of a Sao Paolo favela.

Such experiences, as the saying goes, often result in "character building", enabling one to tap hidden reserves of strengths while even acquiring new skills, and there is little doubt that this has happened for us too. But the truth is that we are getting rather weary of building our (respective or collective) characters at present and, notwithstanding my ever-increasing dexterity with the fly swatter and various substitutes, I would vastly prefer directing my hand-eye efforts to hitting tennis balls in a decidedly more urban environment.

Yes, there is scenery. There is a glut, a surfeit, a preponderance of captivating landscape. And there is the weather: good weather—indeed, great weather. And perhaps, if we weren't so overwhelmingly mired with guilt at the prospect of sending our children into a mindless abyss on a daily basis, we might well be able to do what one really should do in this part of the world during some well-earned time away—hike, read, reflect and relax, while largely avoiding contact with the natives whose presence can be relied upon to add a splash of "colour" now and then. But we are not, *hélas*, in such a situation.

So we're thinking, at present, of relocating again in January. Based upon a number of factors, including your various recommendations, we're currently considering Lyon, and are motivated to drive up and check it out during the Toussaint school break at the end of October. Thoughts? Help?

Beseechingly yours,

Howard

Francophilia

September 30, 2007

Dear N & L,

Thanks very much for the recently-received care package. The exceptionally thoughtful literary books for the children are very much appreciated indeed, as was the heartfelt card.

Regarding the card, however, it occurs to me that, based on your tone, you may feel we are feeling rather overwhelmingly despondent about things. Perhaps, you may even wonder, we are spending our time indulging in forlorn, self-pitying sentiments that sometimes involve wishing we had never come to France at all (i.e "DON'T GIVE UP", "*Voilà mes renforts*", "*J'espère que vous ne serez pas trop déçus*", and so forth). Let me put your minds at ease. No.

No, no, no, no, no.

NO.

Today marks the end of the sixth week since we arrived here, and I can say without hesitation that, all told, the experience has been exactly what we desired—indeed, if anything, slightly superior to what we had expected. True, we have had our various bureaucratic battles with banks, *France Telecom* and so forth, but that was hardly unforeseen and, in fact, considerably less arduous than what I had expected (it helps to have one's expectations appropriately low, of course).

True too, the French countryside (or at least our little slice of it) does not appear to be inundated with *savants* and *érudits* behind every tree anxious to pop out to discuss the finer aspects of the Hegelian dialectic (*Tant mieux,* in this particular case). *Quelle surprise.* Our children's educational institutions are hardly of international calibre, and in fact do represent our primary issue of concern, but, it is important to put things in their proper perspective and recognize that, as you yourselves have said, the entire *point* of this year's educational activity—at least the formal part—was to give the kids an opportunity to really become fluent in French. All the other stuff—math, history, geography and so forth—we could certainly handle independently.

I realize that many of your concerns about our welfare might well be traced back to these weekly updates I am spewing forth, which hardly come across as unequivocally positive reports of our experiences here. It must be admitted that I am occasionally guilty of over-emphasizing matters for dramatic effect, and that as a result I sometimes resort to dwelling on the negative for inappropriately long periods of time.

Relatedly, it is also true that unsavoury experiences (bureaucratic idiocy, frustratingly low educational standards, general living conditions and so forth) do have a tendency to rather more forcefully intrude on one's consciousness than positive ones, which tend to be more quietly absorbed and sometimes require a more substantial period of time before one is even fully aware of them.

Your rather alarmist reaction in your recent card did force me to undergo a quick rereading of my recent letters, however; and after some reflection it does indeed seem clear to me that they were rather top-heavy (bottom-heavy?) with negative sentiments, thereby potentially painting a fairly inaccurate picture of our general frame of mind.

Allow me, then, to take the opportunity to rectify matters somewhat by honestly expounding on why I am perfectly delighted to be here.

Five things I love about France:

1) The beauty

This country is simply *saturated* with beauty. Urban/rural, village/city, hills, ravines, gorges, mountains, beaches, the list just goes on and on. From our all-too-typical little village in Languedoc we are surrounded by beautiful things at every turn. Having been mired for some time in a Canadian locale that was not only exceptionally ugly (or, as Lisa Rochon of the Globe and Mail once so pithily put it, "a city of surpassing ugliness") but, even worse, *unnecessarily* ugly (i.e. hardly being geographically or economically confined to cleaning up the local mine or handling toxic waste), the opportunity to be somewhere where aesthetic considerations are significantly and seamlessly incorporated into one's lifestyle is a daily treat.

Because it's worth stressing that the French sense of the aesthetic goes considerably beyond prudent government regulations that outlaw tacky highway signs for discount furniture warehouses—there seems to be a clear sense throughout the land that their bounteous natural environment should be actively enjoyed, maintained and respected. The remarkable system of *Grandes Randonnées* that provide a plethora of stunning, well-maintained hiking trails that criss-cross the country is the universal gold standard invoked by outdoor enthusiasts everywhere, but what sometimes goes overlooked is the millions of smaller, more intimate trails that wind through virtually every corner of each *département*, developed and maintained by a region, municipality or village.

Every corner of the country is catalogued by a series of detailed topographical maps developed by the *Institut Géographique National* and easily available for sale throughout the land. Most sporting goods stores have extensive departments for hiking and outdoor activities. In France, unlike anywhere else I've ever been, there is a strong sense that the relationship to the land is a sacred trust, that every citizen somehow shares the opportunity to participate in and has an obligation to safeguard the surrounding countryside. Other nations (certainly including Canada) give a significant amount of lip-service to these sorts of sentiments, but in France they appear to be genuinely taken seriously by the vast majority of the citizenry. Hikers are hardly continually besieged by ugly signs despoiling the landscape urging them to clean up after themselves and threatened with the prospects of steep fines for littering. Nobody litters. Nobody even ***thinks*** about littering - and this in a place where the outdoor picnic is almost obligatory. After all, who in his right mind would simply throw used candy wrappers into his own back yard?

2) The intellectual liveliness

So this may surprise you given my various lamentations on the cerebral shortcomings of my fellow *Pougétois*, but it really shouldn't—I hardly expected much from the locals here, after all (although the lack of any outdoor chess game is still, I must confess, a bit of a sticking point—as is the worrying fact that I have yet to see any *Pougétois* immersed in the act of reading anything, even *bandes dessinées*).

But every morning, upon dropping Louis off at his Gignac penitentiary, I begin my journey back to my rural idyll by spending half an hour or so listening to *France Culture*, merrily immersing myself in a number of spirited debates about this and that issue of the day. True, it is sometimes pretentious and it also must be admitted that I don't always manage to capture every word of what is being said, but I usually manage to get the gist of things, at least. As far as the pretentiousness factor goes, as I've said on many occasions, it is far better to be pretentious than to not aspire to anything at all.

Moreover, there are often several moments of genuine, meaningful, informative exchange.

The other day, for example, I was listening to former politician Lionel Jospin being interviewed by the usual coterie of talking heads about his controversial new book. One of the heads, some woman, politely and respectfully asked him why he had written the book—i.e. what he was hoping to accomplish by penning it (other than buttressing his reputation and ego, one could palpably infer).

Overjoyed with joy, I excitedly stepped on the accelerator and nearly slammed into the meandering *vendange* truck in front of me. Finally! A writer being forced to cogently respond to a penetrating question posed by an interlocutor who has an IQ considerably greater than that of your average houseplant! No softball questions lobbed merrily towards the author asking him to explain how he could possibly have found the time to write so many words given his busy schedule, or beseeching him to read an excerpt out loud for the (presumably illiterate) audience. No. A discussion involving the author and people who clearly read the damn thing ahead of time and, moreover, know something about the issues.

And *France Culture,* while doubtless impressive, is hardly the only informative radio station on the dial. There is the often-stimultating *France Inter*, the chatty *France Info*, the remarkably-varied *France Musique* (where one is liable to hear a Beethoven violin sonata, Bob Marley and Georges Brassens in rapid succession). Almost every night on television there is an interesting documentary about something or other that is not continually interrupted by commercial breaks.

Meanwhile, as you well know there is a plethora of engaging and well-written newspapers here all across the political spectrum, replete with articles by people who have challenging and sometimes provocative views that they regularly put forward in an articulate, thoughtful, and often amusing manner.

Lastly, there is this single incontestable point that encapsulates all that is really necessary to say about the manifold glories of the French intellect: Woody Allen is given his proper due here and recognized as the cinematic genius that he is (sarcastic francophobes will invariably wryly add upon hearing this that Jerry Lewis is also in the French cinematic pantheon, but anecdotal reports have led me to conclude that this is nothing other than an urban myth—or, perhaps more likely still, a rural phenomenon).

3) Their sense of values

So this is related to the above, but is nonetheless different, and really defines why, at the end of the day, I prefer France to England (where intellectual liveliness is also on display in various guises). For all of their periodic bouts of hypocritical posturing, chest-thumping anti-Americanism, often-venal foreign policy and sometimes insufferable xenophobia, the French really **do** take the idea of values seriously and are genuinely intent on creatively structuring/re-structuring a society where there is more to life than simply possessing a fat bank account and a healthy increase in national economic productivity. In short, all of this incessant talk of *les droits* is not simply buffoonery—some of it is, of course—but at its core it is genuinely based on ***something;*** and that something, in my view, is damned important indeed.

The standard Anglospheric reaction to all of this, I recognize, is to claim that the entire French economic and social system is irredeemably broken, that spiteful words of "Anglo-Saxon economic hegemony" are nothing more than bitter expressions of envy by a once-global power futilely determined to somehow reassert itself on the international stage, and that, sooner or later, the French will just have to "accept reality" and become "like everybody else" (i.e. 'us').

While fully recognizing that there is much about France's structure that definitely needs shaking up, I must confess that I regard this superficial, condescending perspective, in all of its *USA Today*-inspired rigour as lying squarely between the specious and the downright inane.

There are many ways to launch a reasoned counterattack here, but perhaps the simplest and most effective way to make the all-too-obvious point that there is more to heaven and earth than is dreamt of by untrammelled capitalism is to highlight the findings from *The Economist*'s own studies.

Every so often, interspersed between their omnipresent rants detailing how France must restructure or die a slow and agonizing death (dire warnings, it should be stressed, that have been repeatedly invoked for at least twenty years now—as I have been a regular reader of the magazine—and quite likely a good deal longer than that), *The Economist* polls its own correspondents to ask where they would prefer to live. Invariably the winning country is...France (typically followed by Italy—another egregious financial mess of even greater proportions). That little tidbit of information hardly provides incontrovertible evidence for my claims of the broad-based superiority of the French approach to life, I appreciate, but then again, I don't think that it's entirely meaningless either.

In short, the difference between France and the Anglosphere seems to be simply this: The French regard the marriage of capitalism and market forces as a means to an end—that is, as (probably) the best way of ensuring civil liberties and economic opportunity for its citizenry so as to allow for society to maximally flourish (production of great art, scientific discovery and so forth).

Certainly, there is much hypocrisy and venality throughout the French political and economic system, and I would expect that their *dirigiste* mentality has invariably led to more corruption, less transparency, and more of an "old boys network" than one would find in more rigorously competitive locales around the globe. This can be, of course, quite problematic (without even touching on obvious economic issues of concern such as how one gives reasonable opportunity for unemployed youths in the *banlieues*). But that doesn't diminish from my fundamental point here. It seems obvious to me that the vast majority of the French still consciously resonate with the basic belief that capitalism exists *for* society to prosper, rather than the increasing view of the Anglosphere, which seems to be quite the other way around.

4) The language

I really love this language—it is wonderfully expressive, elegant, witty and spectacularly beautiful. Of course, I don't have nearly the command of it that I would like at present, but that just means that my appreciation for it will only increase as time elapses. Moreover, I very much enjoy the fact that there clearly exists, in some quarters anyway, a sentiment that it is important to speak the language ***well***—which is to say, not just competently or sufficiently—e.g. so that one can request the correct toilet seat at *Monsieur Bricolage* or order the appropriate dish at a restaurant—but to speak precisely and thoughtfully in order to best evoke the desired images and concepts, which naturally necessitates a full grasp of the appropriate grammar, required idioms and vocabularly.

As I get older I become increasingly convinced of the non-trivial link between speaking and thinking; and another in the long line of things that I find infuriating about North America is not only that English is not spoken particularly well, but far worse still, there doesn't even seem to be an awareness that this inability might be an issue of concern—most of the time, in fact, when I try to point this out to people they furrow their brows at me with bemused miscomprehension, as if I am questioning the point of hockey's offside rule.

England, it is true, is much better about this sort of thing (it is hard to imagine *Eats, Shoots & Leaves*, to take but one example, coming forth from the linguistically indifferent wilderness of North America), but then living there forces one to regularly deal with so much other tediousness (rampaging class structure, gloomy weather, football hooligans, island insularity) I'm not sure it really makes up for it at the end of the day. And it is also true that the English are clearly sliding, rather precipitously, towards the completely utilitarian approach to their language that so vividly characterizes their North American colinguists. Advertisements on The Tube used to be filled with clever wordplay. Nowadays, their consumption-urging slogans are just like those in New York.

The French, meanwhile, still seem almost obsessed with their language. Game shows are littered with questions on *"conjugaison"* and *"vocabulaire"* while the unveiling of the latest *Littré* is regarded as a nationally significant event. I'm not sure if you're as up to date on these things as you might otherwise be given your naturally Canadian worldview these days, but recently the French writer Patrick Rambaud came out with a new book entitled *La Grammaire en s'amusant*, adamantly averring that comprehension of the structural details of the language was necessary for French youth to fully comprehend the world around them, and that navigating the subtleties of French grammar could be "more fun than a video game".

Whether one agrees or disagrees with this sentiment, it is hard to deny the obvious importance the French bestow on developing an appropriate command of their language. It is also hard to imagine how such a book would ever get published in North America, let alone read.

Anyway, I love French. I love the rhythms, the cadence, the metaphors and the expressiveness of the language. It is not easy, even though I have a reasonable enough grounding of the basics, but sometimes it is good to do something difficult, to challenge oneself at a fundamental level; and for the likes of me, there is little more fundamental—and, correspondingly potentially frustrating—than not being able to express myself as clearly as I might like. But I can't help but feel that the whole experience is definitely good for me, and I well recognize that now is the perfect opportunity to engage in this ambitious and rewarding task.

5) Being left alone

This may seem like a strange feature to highlight in my encapsulation of my own personal sense of the glories of *La*

France, but it must be said that I very much enjoy the fact that there seems to be a clear sense of privacy and reserve in the French that just allows one to simply **be**. Whether I'm waiting at the school to pick up Emmy or strolling through a Montpellier bookstore, people have this wonderful ability to simply *leave you the hell alone*.

Perhaps I'm being over-sensitive, but I can't help but feel that, at least in North America, people generally feel compelled to bother you, invade your personal space, waste your time, ask you if you've found everything you were looking for (who the hell ever finds ***that***, by the way?), have a nice day or some other inanity. Here, on the other hand, there is a decided awareness of the sanctity of one's personal space, both literal and metaphorical. Even the friendly, (unfairly?) ridiculed local villagers, respectfully keep their distance, sensitive to one's sense of privacy and naturally concerned about imposing.

True, as we personally experienced, this heightened sense of privacy does run the risk of resulting in periods of awkward tension for those who, unintentionally or otherwise, invade it (e.g. walking across someone's property without explicit permission) but that is simply a case of knowing, and respecting, the rules.

And then, relatedly, there is the whole issue of money and the increasingly cavalier way most North Americans seem to unhesitatingly probe one's personal finances, something which is thankfully regarded as rather gauche and déclassé in these parts.

Had I taken a year off and gone to the US, say, I'm certain I would have been subjected to incessant questions from curious onlookers about my future employment prospects, the price of homes, how precisely we are planning on supporting ourselves in the longer term, and all of that.

Over here, on the other hand, you mention to people that you have opted to indulge in an *année sabbatique* and the response is invariably straightforward head-nodding and general understanding. "Taking some time off, then, are you?" they respond. "Well, good for you. That's what life is all about." Indeed.

In conclusion, then, *ne vous inquiétez pas*. I am really very happy here and there is nowhere else I would rather be (well no other country, anyway).

Francophilically yours,

Howard

Going Native (slowly)

October 7, 2007

Dear N & L,

We live, as the Chinese are reputed to cryptically say with some regularity, in interesting times.

This past week began with both Irena and myself becoming slowly yet steadily consumed by the growing drumbeat of despair that is naturally associated with the increasing awareness (and concomitant feelings of guilt) of having summarily dumped our children in the equivalent of educational purgatory.

By Thursday evening, buffeted by the daily ritual of picking up our despondent children, we had come to the conclusion that the whole Languedoc immersion experience simply wasn't working and it was time to simply yank them out of their pernicious scholastic environments and investigate other alternatives, come what may.

First, however, we had to tackle yet another barrage of unsavoury administrative tasks on Friday in nearby Montpellier. Montpellier is, as you are probably well aware, a bit of an odd place. The old centre is unquestionably charming and engaging, replete with beautiful old buildings along wending cobblestone streets that seamlessly integrate the classic with the modern, yet the outlying areas which ring the old city are almost uniformly dingy and unappealing. The University of Montpellier, with its celebrated medical school, has long been a star in the international educational firmament (I believe Petrarch studied law there), yet these days the principal academic areas are quite removed from the centre which seems almost exclusively geared to shopping and tourists (of which there are zillions, particularly in the summer). It is obviously a growing city, doubtlessly propelled by its enviable southern location, with construction going on virtually everywhere, but seemingly in an incoherent, almost random manner.

Infrastructure is a curious combination of very good and very bad. The public transportation system of trams appears to be both modern and efficient, while numerous convenient and easily accessible underground parking lots have been constructed to accommodate even the mighty hordes who descend each summer. On the other hand, there is, rather bizarrely, no real "ring road", so that anytime one wishes to drive around the city en route to anywhere else, one is forced to confront endless suburban roundabouts and sit in lengthy traffic queues on inappropriately narrow roads.

Our first destination was the airport to retrieve some additional bags that my mother had graciously shipped over. We drove down with some trepidation, convinced that French officialdom would force us to provide them with an itemized list of the contents (which we didn't have), our *cartes de séjour* (which we still don't possess), or some other as yet still-uncontemplated document that eluded our wildest bureaucratic dreams/nightmares.

In a desperate effort to prepare ourselves for the bureaucratic unknown, we equipped nonetheless with passports, driver's licences (Ontario and Dutch), our rental contract, bills from *France Telecom* addressed to us in Le Pouget, sundry bills addressed to our Canadian address, copies of our marriage certificate, photographs of the children and sundry other documents that vaguely testify to our existence on planet earth.

An hour and a half and several dozen roundabouts later, we managed to locate the Air France Cargo outlet, a facility that has all of the imposing presence as that of the Le Pouget post office, which we discovered was manned by one lonely fellow in a small poorly lit room who was immersed in a crossword puzzle.

I introduced myself and he seemed particularly pleased to see me, from which I could only surmise that I was one of the very few customers he had this week (month? year?). As I thumbed through the labyrinth of our accompanying paperwork to see which document I should provide to identify myself, he hurriedly pressed two sheets of paper into my hand and told me to go upstairs to talk to customs. Vaguely disappointed that I still remained officially unidentified (you see what this place does to you?), we mounted the stairs to penetrate the customs office—here, presumably, the real fuss would start.

We entered another room that was unoccupied save for a back office where two kindly middle-aged ladies were engaged in a discussion, while a small dog scurried about. The dog, having spied us, rushed over to greet us while we were left uncertain as to how to proceed (Knock on the counter? Gradually raise our voices to higher auditory levels? Cough loudly?). In the end, I elected to simply pick up the dog and play with it, thereby demonstrating my palpable Canadian friendliness together with a potentially eye-catching manoeuvre to attract the necessary attention from the authorities.

Some five minutes later, one of the ladies eventually noticed us—or perhaps the lack of the dog in her orbit—meandered over and apologized profusely for the delay, asked us whether or not we liked France and unthinkingly stamped our documents. All of this while her interlocutor came over and repossessed the dog, shaking her head while informing us that he was hardly the sort of beast that belongs in a customs office, given his propensity for merrily going off with *n'importe qui*. Maybe, the other laughingly suggested, they should try training him to sniff for drugs and contraband instead.

I smiled wanly, inwardly charmed by the situation but still very much instinctively terrified after so many years of waiting in airport queues reading signs sharply informing me that *ANY PERSON WHO MENTIONS FIREARMS, SMUGGLING OR NARCOTICS IN THE PRESENCE OF A CUSTOMS OFFICIAL IS SUBJECTED TO IMMEDIATE SEARCH AND LIKELY INCARCERATION.* At any rate, five minutes later, we were back downstairs with the sleepy Air France Cargo man who glanced briefly at our customs stamp, asked us to pay 42 Euros as part of the ubiquitously mysterious "airport tax" and promptly hauled out our bags to the nearby loading dock before returning, presumably, to the land of crossword puzzles, exhausted after fully utilizing his customer-service skills for the week. The whole thing took perhaps 10 minutes, and most of that was spent playing with the dog.

Of course, this bureaucratic smoothness would not last. From there, your intrepid correspondents marched off into the bowels of administrative hell—straight into the heart of the Montpellier *Mobistore* where I was now a quasi-regular, having been there twice before already (once to order my phone line and discuss various internet "package" possibilities and another time to officially sign my fancy "internet contract" with *livebox*—the fancy apparatus, I'm led to believe, that actually allows one to use an ADSL connection with one's computer).

Some background, sadly, is required here. As I believe I already mentioned to you in a previous missive, unbeknownst to me at the time, the *France Telecom* technicians had not actually installed an ADSL phone line when they connected us (on *The Day of the Decapitated Bunny,* you may recall), leaving me unable to use any of the home internet apparatus that duly arrived by courier several days after *The Signing of the Big Contract* (What is it with French bureaucrats and the act of signing contracts, by the way? They treat the whole experience with so much pomp and circumstance, I always feel drastically underdressed whenever I sign anything).

I discovered this, as it happens, when I tried to connect my *livebox* and found that its automatic diagnostic check kept stalling at the "check ADSL line" stage—no fool, I. Frustrated, I phoned the friendly woman at the *Mobistore* ("you can always phone me if you have any problems" she had cheerily informed me during *The Signing of the Big Contract*) and explained my issues before suggesting that perhaps the *France Telecom* guys had somehow not installed an ADSL line after all given my difficulties, requesting that perhaps she might phone them on my behalf to verify matters.

She breezily replied that she thought that highly unlikely, that the order was well and truly in her computer (?!), that the contract was, of course, signed (?!), and that in any event she certainly couldn't phone *France Telecom* because they were a completely different organization. She coolly recommended that I phone the *Orange* service number (*Orange,* the service provider, is also, needless to say, a completely different organization) displayed prominently on my documents if I was having any difficulty in following the installation instructions.

Well. At this point, I began to appreciate that I was dealing with forces that were well and truly beyond my powers, and decided that, under the circumstances it might be best if I could find someone else to phone the aforementioned number on my behalf—partially because I hoped that some of the difficulty might be traced to my French, but also because it wasn't clear that I had the necessary social skills to handle the looming conflict and I might just ruin any future chance for a phone line by having an excoriating exchange with these bozos—discretion being the better part of valour and all of that.

So I arranged for a French acquaintance of ours to do the dirty deed. Unfortunately, her level of technical expertise makes me look positively Edisonian by comparison (a difficult feat, I can assure you) and so I had to run through the entire (aborted) installation process several times in her presence before she felt she had the necessary knowledge to grapple with the service line (thereby soundly defeating the purpose of engaging a native speaker to begin with).

Eventually, not without some trepidation, she made the call and discovered that…yes indeed, *France Telecom* had **not** installed an ADSL line (without, needless to say, bothering to inform me), although matters were naturally complicated by the fact that the service line was not *France Telecom*'s per se but rather *Orange's*, whose technicians were good enough to place us on hold for half an hour (during which time, *bien sûr*, we kept paying by the minute for the call) while they contacted *France Telecom*.

We were eventually informed that, notwithstanding our initial assumptions, it was *impossible* to get ADSL service in Le Pouget. When I replied, via my French phone friend, that this was somewhat perplexing given the fact that the previous occupant of **this very house** had indeed had precisely such a line several months ago before cancelling it when he trekked off to Washington; and that, moreover, the *Mobistore* had apparently pre-cleared the whole business with *France Telecom* ahead of time, we were subjected to another lengthy pause to appropriately verify matters while, presumably, more technicians ruminated. Or something.

Eventually, in true Delphic fashion, the answer came wafting back to us: Yes, indeed, there **had** been some ADSL service in Le Pouget, but unfortunately the ADSL capacity is now "*saturé*".

Unable to control myself at this incomprehensible turn of events, I exploded with: *"What the hell does **that** mean?"*— which, needless to say, merely resulted in me being subjected to a condescending response on the definition of what "saturated" means, which hardly addressed my confusion. To put it rather mildly.

To make matters worse, it appeared irritatingly uncertain when *France Telecom* would even be able to ***ascertain*** when (if?) ADSL capacity in Le Pouget would somehow become desaturated, although we were blithely informed that they would "try to get back to us eventually and hopefully within a week or so".

A week or so later, the news came to us from on high that, ADSL capacity in Le Pouget is truly ***saturé*** for the indefinite future.

At this point, a curious shift in my perspective mysteriously presented itself, as I began wondering why on Earth I was so intent on having home internet service anyway. After years of being surrounded on all sides by people continually intent on instantaneously replying to incoming email barrages, unthinkingly reducing their attention spans to gnat-like proportions as they scurried hither and thither like headless chickens, emailing each other frantically from their toilet stalls during bathroom breaks from their endless series of mindless meetings, might it not be better to finally take a different approach to communication much more in keeping with my newly-discovered thoughtful and measured life perspective?

Indeed, I reflected, perhaps the entire affair was actually all part of some master plan—a necessary detox sentence cleverly bestowed upon me by the all-knowing *État*, resolutely determined to safeguard my **droit de penser**.

And so my thoughts abruptly turned from how to get the *livebox* to work to how to get rid of the damned thing. Another trip to Montpellier, I sadly recognized, would still be necessary to once again explain the situation, annul the contract and move resolutely forwards towards an internet-free life.

So here, after this lengthy digression, we pick up the thread of my narrative once more, fresh from the rapid conquest of Air France Cargo and the friendly customs canine.

I arrived at the Mobistore with *livebox* in tow, determined to explain our situation for the last time. Half an hour later, after the now fully expected administrative response of disbelief and confusion followed by sundry phone calls spent in verifying the details of my story, we were informed that, *hélas*, I couldn't drop off my *livebox* there, but must give it back to a *France Telecom* office.

Moreover, the onus was apparently on me to send a detailed letter, by registered mail no less, to the *Orange* head office in Bordeaux fully explaining the situation, complete with various photocopies of the contract and a receipt from *France Telecom* proving that I had actually returned the *livebox*.

It was at this point that, hitherto firmly united against the Administrative Hydra, Irena and I began to part company.

GOING NATIVE (SLOWLY)   93

While I nodded matter-of-factly to this latest series of absurdities, fully determined to completely ignore the request, Irena kept pestering our agent for more detailed information: *Where should we send the letter to, exactly? What should we say? When should we send it?* I fixed her with a stony glare, determined to transparently transmit my message of *If you think I'm going to spend one more minute in engaging in this asinine business once I've purged myself of this god-damned livebox, you are sadly mistaken* to the very best of my abilities, but she was unswayed. *Might you*, she respectively requested the stalwart *Mobistorette*, *be so good as to compose the letter yourself for us, given our poor French literary skills*?

From here, after a few aborted attempts involving me taking dictation from this girl while trying to contain my irritation at participating in this most absurd of all possible tasks, we eventually moved to a scenario where the *Mobistorette* penned the letter, while I occupied myself with evaluating her orthographical abilities (*Shouldn't that have an accent grave? I don't use accents. Shouldn't "Bordeaux" have an "x" on the end? Um, yes, I think you're right).*

Upon leaving the store, I immediately turned angrily upon Irena: "What the hell was **that** all about? You're not seriously thinking about sending this letter are you?" It seemed, strangely, she was.

"I don't want to get in trouble with *France Telecom*", she countered firmly. "If we don't do what they tell us to do, they might boot us out of the country."

This is, needless to say, precisely how all totalitarian regimes derive their power over their citizenry.

The story took one final turn towards the ridiculous when we made our way to the nearest *France Telecom* office and, faced with the inevitable unmoving queue, I began playing around with the vacant computers nonchalantly placed in the middle of the store (trying to check my email, as it happened). Eventually, a password-protected message leapt forth and, after trying a few random possibilities, shut down the program. After a few more minutes of non-service, we were about to leave the *agence* when a *France Telecom* person arrived, but our joy at the prospect of some form of attention turned to despair when she resolutely placed herself in front of the aforementioned computer in the middle of the store and started typing away, oblivious to all concerned. After a few minutes of this she grew frustrated and bellowed: "Who touched my computer?!"

Given that the other would-be customers in the queue had possibly witnessed my oh-so-public technological derring-do, I eventually thought it would be best to fess up to my terroristic exploits (Who could have possibly known that it was ***her*** computer, placed as it was right in the centre of a small office in plain view of everyone? Certainly not me.), but naturally elected to leave shortly thereafter to try my hand at returning my *livebox* at another FT *bureau*. Dealing with *France Telecom* was difficult enough under relatively benign circumstances, I hated to even contemplate what might befall us should we have to deal with someone there who had it in for us at the beginning of the exchange.

But the most noteworthy aspect of the day's experiences was quite unrelated to our administrative peregrinations and was instead surprisingly political in nature. You know well that I have long been intrigued by the French political scene, which I have always found highly entertaining—a curious mélange of idealism, pragmatism, opportunism, bombast, insularity, arrogance, self-indulgence, wit and gobbledygook (with the typical craven capitulation to the omnipresent *manifestation* thrown in for good measure).

Now, of course, with Monsieur Sarkozy in power and the political earth shifting behind everyone's feet with people of all political stripes suddenly finding themselves in powerful positions and a manic triangulation occurring that is orders of magnitude greater than the Clintonian standard of yore, it is easily the most exciting show in town.

So over the past few weeks Irena and I have watched various political talk shows and engaged in several animated discussions about what seems to be going on here, politically-speaking. But what I had not at all appreciated, however, was that younger family members might be paying the slightest bit of attention to any of this.

So it was that the other day, as I was driving Louis to Collège, he informed me that his school was presently engaged in the activity of selecting class *délégués* for the student government. He began the discussion by complaining about the fact that the requisite information session would result in him staying at school an extra hour on Friday afternoon, but I quickly rebutted this position by slipping in to my well-worn role of tedious parental pedant.

Stop complaining, I chastised him. Now's your chance to discover if these guys actually take this whole business of *le droit* seriously. Find out, I encouraged him, what the rights and responsibilities of class delegates really are—what they can and can't do and how they can actually improve the student experience. See what's really going on and if it's more than just hot air.

And then, as usual, I promptly forgot all about it.

But Louis didn't, it seems. While his mother and I were bombarding him with sundry issues in history, mathematics and grammar, a political plot of sorts was clearly hatching in his mind. Thursday night before he went to bed, he informed us that he was going to stand for election in Friday's election as class *délégué* and had been secretly preparing his speech. This was truly amazing. The child seems to have no knowledge of the fact that a reasonable prerequisite for political office of any sort is some sort of mastery of the language of communication. Still, one can't help but admire his determination and intestinal fortitude—*Il a du toupet, ce gosse.* Bloody unstoppable.

I thought about giving him the standard fatherly patronizing speech commending him on his initiative but urging him to be reasonable and leave this first election to others, thereby sparing him the inevitable crushing defeat and the consequent deluge of tormenting barbs from his fellow school ruffians, but at the end of the day I opted not to. I can't change his mind anyway (a source, as you might imagine, of considerable pride to me), and maybe at the end of the day he was right.

Perhaps this flagrant show of courage would somehow earn him the respect of some of his more Neandertholic colleagues and enable him to integrate better in his surroundings, like trying out for the school football team being 30 pounds underweight and coming away from the experience with three broken limbs but spared from considerable further taunting.

Well, you probably guessed what happened. He won. When we picked him up Friday afternoon, exhausted after our various bloody administrative battles, he greeted us with an enormous smile, jumping up and down and going on excitedly about his "killer speech" and his enthusiastic plans for making 6B the most progressive class in Gignac academic history (likely not that difficult, all things considered, but still…).

After dinner that night, he re-enacted his successful speech for us. It was a grammatical nightmare of epic proportions; and yet the essential points came through loud and clear: playing on the theme of the "outsider", mocking the specious and perverting notion of high school popularity, he trumpeted the notions of *égalité, fraternité* and *les droits* all the way to the proverbial bank and won in a landslide.

I will spare you the hypocritical homilies about how delighted I am to be proven wrong by my child and learn life lessons from him. The truth is that I don't enjoy being proven wrong by anyone and certainly not my eleven-year-old son. Moreover, I would never give him the satisfaction of knowing that he might have something to teach me—he is reticent enough as is to believe that I might occasionally have something to say worth listening to and I well appreciate the time is fast approaching when he will resolutely ignore with a condescending sneer any and all words of wisdom that I wish to impart to him.

But all of this *does* rather pose a problem for your intrepid travelers. Just as Irena and I had firmly resolved to write off the Languedocian experience and head towards more civilized parts of the country (i.e. anywhere), we find ourselves in the perplexing position of having children who are suddenly showing distinct signs of settling in. For we later learned that on the same Friday afternoon when Louis was catapulting himself to higher political office, his sister was busy overwhelming people during a soccer game in gym class. It appears that girls do not regularly engage in *le foot* in Languedoc, and the fact that shy, retiring Emmy managed to reduce legions of pursuing boys (and teachers) to rubble has recently earned her nothing less than iconic status throughout her school.

So there it is. It now seems hard to deny that moving to another locale just as our children are reaping the fruits of their integrationist labours would smack of undue selfishness; and so we have decided to backtrack on our recent resolutions and somehow try to stick it out here for a while longer after all.

But…we've also decided that a year is really not sufficient to be in these parts (not the least of which because it forces one to be constantly thinking of next steps and not productively enjoy the moment) and are currently resolved that, unless something unexpected happens, we will somehow try to stay in France for at least the next couple of years, taking advantage of the months ahead to scout out appropriate locations and opportunities for the longer term (Lyon? Aix-en-Provence? Marseille? Paris?). It's really a very nice country you have here—it's quite a shame for you that you let me convince you to leave it. More fool you.

At any rate, that's the plan of the day—hopefully it won't change again drastically next week. Stay tuned...

Vacillatingly yours,

Howard

On The Ground

October 14, 2007

Dear N & L,

A calm week for once, filled with reflection and contemplation of our environs, given that we have—for the moment, anyway—concluded that it would be best to stick it out here now that the children are showing distinct signs of adjusting to their surroundings.

In keeping with this resolution, I have logically elected to focus on the strengths of the area and turned inwards, Thoreau-like, and become, you may be amused to know, ***nature man***—exploring much of the surrounding area by foot after having boldly made the trip to a nearby sporting goods store to indulge in a fit of uncharacteristic consumerism to purchase a pair of hiking shoes.

There is, of course, much to see. A few obvious points to mention—or at least points that probably should have been obvious, but somehow took us by surprise nonetheless, given how little background research we did on the area before coming:

There's a real fall here. Much of the surrounding vegetation turns various impressive colours—pale yellow, warm golden, orange, crimson and even purple—including, most spectacularly and unexpectedly, the vineyards, which all obligingly turn precisely the same hue in giant rectangular chunks, presumably depending on the particular type of grape being harvested on each field (Allotment? Meadow? *vendange carré*?). My favourite walk that I regularly indulge in just before picking Emmy up for her lunchtime break from school involves meandering past the village and up along a nearby ridge where I can sample a delightful 360° view of the surrounding countryside, complete with all the different shades of nearby vineyards, glinting like a patchwork quilt in the Mediterranean sun.

Said sun, you may be jealous to hear given the rather wet and frosty conditions I imagine you are now subjected to on a not infrequent basis, is still intent on shining brightly and warmly. While daybreak can definitely be on the cool side (generally no more than 5° or so), by mid-afternoon the temperature is typically hovering somewhere in the mid-twenties, often making it a bit too warm to seriously consider strenuous outdoor activity at this time—hence my determination to hike in the late morning instead. As it happens, given my general preference for indulging in other aspects of my isolationist agenda in the early hours, this is not actually my preferred time for a stroll, but we all have to make sacrifices, I suppose, and adapt to the constraints of our situation. Furthermore, I'm told that December and January present perfect mid-afternoon hiking conditions, so that is something to look forward to.

There is also, it should be added, a decidedly impressive amount of variety in the local terrain. A mere fifteen-minute drive from our house, for example, takes one to the painfully charming village of Mourèze, the north end of which abuts a spectacularly eerie jumble of dolomitic rocks, some as high as dozens of metres, in a setting not completely unlike what one might find in the wilds of Arizona or Montana. Beyond the rocks, meanwhile, looms the impressive bowl-like southern face of the *Montagne de Liausson* (the principal mountainous star, it should be clarified, of our nightly back porch sunset show), that gives rise to the famed *Cirque de Mourèze*. A vigorous hike through the boulder field up to the top of the Liausson ridge, meanwhile, gives one access to stunning views of not only the *Cirque* below, but also the expansive *Lac du Salagou* on the other side. And all of this while perpetually bathed in the remarkable regional light; and moreover, quite often without encountering **one** single, solitary person to interrupt one's appreciation of the physical beauty or sense of communing with nature—nothing but the chattering of birds and the sound of the wind through the cypress trees. Truly outstanding.

Meanwhile, daily indoor life has begun to quietly (once again quietly, mercifully quietly) settle into a rather productive routine, so much so that I am having a hard time remembering how I found time to do anything interesting at all during the days when I was regularly employed (perhaps—gasp!—I didn't). I have recently started working away on a (hopefully) comic novel that I am having great fun with, revelling in being liberated from the tiresome constraints of reality that my previous non-fictional efforts were (necessarily) saddled with—far more enjoyable to write about what should have happened somewhere/somehow than what actually did.

When the kids come back from school in the late afternoon, I generally spend time playing games with them before Irena and I hunker down to help them with their homework. Most of their exercises are both dreary and uninspiring, as is so often the case everywhere, but there are the odd exceptions that typically involve something uniquely French.

I have lately, for example, developed a passionate fondness for the various *chansons* they are charged with learning and plunge into the task of memorizing the words and music with great vigour. Louis and I have become quite competent at singing *À La Claire Fontaine* in duet form, for example, while Emmy and I take unbridled delight in marching around the house belting out *La Marseillaise* at the slightest provocation (well, 2 out of the 6 verses, anyway, plus the refrain), much to the chagrin of Irena, who must at times feel very much like an oppressed general of the Prussian army.

Otherwise, I am tinkering away on the piano here with some regularity and am, of course, reading. I have recently vowed, in the spontaneously peremptory fashion that I am sometimes guilty of in my giddier moments, to read only in French for the indefinite future. Much of this, it must be admitted, was triggered by my delighted realization in the middle of a Montpellier bookstore that the more literary strands of French society (which is to say, those who had mastered the ability to read and write, as opposed to our friendly *Pougétois*) had clearly many things to say about Spinoza; and that I could smoothly continue my study of this most insightfully withdrawn iconoclast (and, *bien sûr*, role model) in French just as well as in English. After all, he wrote in Latin anyway (aside from a few things in Dutch). But there is more, of course, than even my beloved Bento: novels, newspapers, magazines—the world of living *en français* in the 21st century beckons; and if I am going to resolutely shun all interaction with any *Homo sapien*s outside of my immediate family, as I am still rather inclined to do at present, then it only makes sense to capitalize on the French experience by some other means.

In the meantime, I find the prospect of relying strictly on French newspapers and magazines for one's regular awareness of global events to be quite a refreshing experience. Canada, unsurprisingly, summarily fades into oblivion—rising above the noise for a passing mention only in the rare instance when the price of some agricultural product (e.g. wheat) or raw material (e.g. oil) it is associated with has suddenly become an issue of French national importance.

The UK has a presence, although not a terribly strong one—rather more as that of a tedious sibling with whom one feels obliged to compare oneself with on significant measures of social progress (unemployment, economic strength and so forth) than as an intrinsically interesting locale in its own right. One hears of comparisons between Sarkozy and Thatcher now and then, but that is typically a mere political barb—antagonistic political rhetoric wafted by his foes on "the left" who are determined to portray him as someone abandoning traditional French values in favour of Anglo-saxon economic hegemony etc, etc.

News about America, on the other hand—economic, social,

political—remains very much front and centre. Be it iPhones or Google, Democratic or Republican primaries, the burst bubble of the American real estate market or the latest Hollywood films, matters American seem to be, somehow, of palpable and direct interest to the French.

So much, so expected, more or less. But then there are the other worlds that abruptly rush into view, places that are either still part of Greater France or once were—Réunion, Mauritius, Guadeloupe, The Seychelles and so on. One suddenly hears about the recent goings on in French-speaking Africa—Chad, Senegal, Côte d'Ivoire and more—that almost never rate even a passing mention with the mainstream North American media.

And then, of course, there is North Africa. I had naturally expected the French to be more sensitive to countries on the other side of the Mediterranean, but almost exclusively oriented towards the issue of immigration to France, social friction, and so forth. Of course, such issues certainly do exist, but there is much, much more. Recently, for example, the peripatetic Sarkozy returned from a whirlwind tour of Algeria, Morocco and Tunisia, signing deals for exporting TGV technology and infrastructure to North Africa and filling the air with talk of a "Pan-Mediterranean Union" based on mutual economic interests. More grandiose political mumbo-jumbo? Quite possibly. But nonetheless certainly different from what I had expected.

Meanwhile, as I bask in my isolationist farmhouse amid the periodic squawking of roosters, trying to get some sense of a geopolitical world-order that is centred on the predilictions of the *Elysée Palace*, Irena is busily occupying herself with *Pougétois* life. In the tiny Friday morning outdoor market in the square next to Emmy's school, she has recently discovered an impressive cheese vendor who not only stocks a wide variety of delectable *fromages*, but also seems to demonstrate a remarkable proficiency as a language instructor.

"Apparently," she relayed to me last Friday in breathless excitement, "A piece of cheese is a '*morceau*' not a '*pièce*'". This tidbit of linguistical culinary precision was followed by a thorough analysis on the various types of camembert, followed by a heartfelt condemnation of any manufacturer who had "sold out" and opted to utilize pasteurized milk in the making of their product. "Our" cheese man, needless to say, only sells the *real* camembert made from *lait cru*.

I suppose I should be on my guard against any man who has so rapidly made such a blazing advance into the heart and mind (not to mention stomach) of my fair wife, but even though she darkly conveys to me that "he speaks so clearly, there's simply no way he's from around here," I still know all too well that there is no cause for alarm. However beguiling he, or his merchandise, might be—there is little chance that Irena will run off with the local cheese man and run the risk of forever trapping herself in the wilds of Languedoc. Or so I console myself, determined as I am to both avoid losing whatever dignity I might still possess by flying into a jealous rage at the alleged machinations of the local travelling cheese vendor—together with, of course, my own weekly fix of chèvre and "real" camembert.

From Irena's various village forays, I have come to learn other news as well.

The *Pougétois*, it appears, are watching *me*!

"Your husband seems to do a lot of walking," one of the villagers slyly mentioned to her as she waited to pick up Emmy from school one day.

"Sometimes", she replied evasively, somewhat taken aback that other people even knew who I was.

But there you go: further proof that we are invariably far more interesting to others than we have any right to be—ah, the exotic appeal of the foreign!

More significantly, there seem to be grand plans afoot to transform the tiny Le Pouget library into a burgeoning *médiatheque*, the decidedly over-exuberant French word that so proudly refers to the evolutionary end-product of the modern library: a locale for surfing the net and signing out DVDs as well as books.

Construction, it seems, on this bold new venture has begun—which is to say that the ground floor of the library is now a disaster area with wires dangling everywhere. Rumour has it that the envisioned end-product is so sweeping in size and scope that Le Pouget will be virtually unrecognizable, unceremoniously thrown firmly into the 21st century (or at least the 20th) with perhaps 10 or 20 (!) computers, all linked with a high-speed network. Irena recently hypothesized that this unique concentration of local technological forces might well have something to do with the fact that all private

ADSL capacity in Le Pouget is now *saturé*—a conclusion which not only struck me as eminently reasonable, but one which naturally brings with it its own modicum of comfort, however cold, to our previous personal email quandaries, elevating our past struggles out of the valley of pointless idiocy and into a far nobler realm where we have somehow (albeit inadvertently) sacrificed our own private high-tech interests to that of the common village good.

From such curious beginnings, stirring tales of sacrifice have been known to begin: *Allons enfants de la Patrie, le jour de surf est arrivé...*

Patriotically yours,

Howard

Restlessness

October 21, 2007

Dear N & L,

Things are, unfortunately, sliding again. Indeed, the lion's share of our time of late has been spent in daily (if not hourly) tacking back and forth between the prospect of sticking things out in Le Pouget or moving somewhere more reasonable (Montpellier, Aix, Lyon, Paris). Such vacillations (*tergiverser, louvoyer*—this is really quite an impressive language you have—you seem to have a word or expression for *everything*) are both tedious and exhausting—one feels rather like one has been treading water for weeks at a time, accomplishing nothing other than merely staying afloat. Barely.

Our principal concern, as always, centres around the kids' schooling, for it seems that our previously established conviction that Louis and Emmy were finally settling in to their surrounding schools was, alas, premature. Or rather, perhaps it is really not an issue of "settling in" after all, but rather more a question of simply "settling"?

It is true that the kids have quite rapidly become used to their "educational environments", daily engaging in their respective daily rituals with nary a complaint, but the question increasingly presents itself: is staying here actually the right thing to be doing for them? After all, given our much-vaunted flexibility, we certainly *could* move elsewhere; and as the full picture of the local experience becomes ever clearer, we are decidedly motivated to at least explore such a scenario.

Emmy's school crawls along with an educational standard geared towards the intellectual acuity of a frying pan, but at least involves a reasonably rigorous treatment of the rudiments of French grammar. Had she actually been a native French speaker, I'm sure she would have become comatose weeks ago at the molasses-like pace of the proceedings, but by some curious coincidence the level of French language pedagogy she is routinely subjected to is quite well suited to an intelligent 10-year-old anglophone, so at least all is not lost on that front. Her teacher, meanwhile, seems like an enormously frustrated fellow, constantly reproaching the class for being "at an extremely low level", threatening all of them with the prospect of (once again?) failing the year, and not infrequently hoisting various spitball-manufacturing *voyous* up by their shirts before dropping them, unceremoniously, onto their desks.

This last point was particularly disconcerting to hear, as you might imagine. At the beginning of the school year, we were steadfastly assured, in a statement that ironically piqued our concern by adamantly denying the absence of things we had long since discounted, that corporal punishment was no longer permitted in the school, presumably because it was against ***le droit*** of the student. One can only surmise that Emmy's teacher found a clever route around the letter, if not the spirit, of this constraint by simply letting gravity (which, I imagine, is imbued with ***le droit*** to make objects fall) do his dirty work for him. Somewhere in all of this pretentious posturing of rights and responsibilities, so far removed from its rightful place as a delineation of the boundaries of a social contract between a state and its citizens, lies something almost sinister—a crutch upon which a failing educational system is desperately relying.

At the same introductory speech denying corporal punishment, for example, we were also informed, rather bizarrely, that the student had the right *not* to do homework—whereupon, presumably, the teacher had the right to fail him, the parents had the right to protest the failure, etc. What the hell is this all about? I remember wondering. *Of course*, the student doesn't *have* to do his homework, and *of course* the teacher can't physically force him to do it. Who in their right minds would ever conclude anything else?

After all, back where I come from there's also no need to conjure up official proclamations that educators are not allowed to force-feed bananas to their students or teach mathematics in the nude, or any other of the virtually infinite number of flatly inappropriate activities to be engaged in within a nominally educational setting.

Wouldn't it be vastly more appropriate to simply recognize that it is the sacred responsibility of the teacher to do whatever she reasonably can, hopefully with the assistance of the parents, to imbue the children with the necessary knowledge (together with, ideally, respect for the learning process itself) so as to become, broadly construed, productive members of society? Isn't that, quite simply, the whole *point* of the entire business? This ain't no postal strike. This is education. Or at least it's supposed to be.

And while Emmy keeps her head down, diligently placing various verbs in their appropriate groups amid the bedlam of ruffians crashing onto their desks, Louis soldiers on stoically, mired in his West Side Story environs without even the benefit of a strong grammatical footing. Which hasn't, interestingly enough, stopped him from rapidly developing considerable verbal dexterity in the local tongue. Ever the impressive mime, he has seamlessly adapted, Jim Carrey-like, to his surroundings, effortlessly spouting forth a stream of expressions in a strong Languedocean accent that often completely eludes our foreign ears.

This is doubtless an accomplishment of sorts, but there is little denying that he seems to have lost a spring in his step. His *délégué* triumph now has the tinge of a distant memory as his comrades have repeatedly ignored his urgings to consider how best to improve their circumstances and have more or less returned to their Neandertholic origins, bullying and tormenting weaker children in emphatic *Lord of the Flies* fashion while surrounding teachers do nothing, presumably buried deep in their Rousseau (relatedly, it has dawned on us that he had profoundly, if sweetly, misinterpreted the role of *délégué*—sincerely believing that he was swept into power with a mandate to change the hearts and minds of his fellow students and lead them to a higher moral plane, rather than the considerably more mundane reality of merely being their official representative at occasional formal gatherings).

In short, the bitter joke that is his "educational environment" no longer seems quite so funny, and as his French has progressed, so has, understandably, his frustration with the general inanity of his circumstances as he gets a clearer and clearer picture of his surroundings. It's high time, methinks, to end this little drama and get him the hell out of there (certainly by Christmas).

But where? Aye, there's the rub. We simply don't know.

And there is also this: I am beginning, slowly, to shake off my feelings of isolationist torpor and feel myself getting ready to engage with the world again. Any remnants of whimsical romantic sentiments of French rural life have well and truly dissipated.

Yes, the scenery is spectacularly beautiful with hiking trails galore. Yes, there is a virtual infinite number of charming villages and quaint little hamlets. Yes, it has been a fascinating experience to see aspects of the *vendange* first hand, as well as witnessing the birth of "snail season" on our back porch. Yes, I have a much keener and more rigorous understanding of the desire to forever freeze the rural landscape that lies at the heart of the hugely distorting subsidies of the EU's Common Agricultural Policy. Yes, yes, yes. BUT I DON'T WANT TO LIVE IN THE MIDDLE OF GOD-DAMNED NOWHERE ANYMORE! My God: I voluntarily moved to a place that makes small town Canada look positively cosmopolitan: What the hell was I ***thinking?***

And, to be frank, it is even worse than I have hitherto let on, determined as I was to dwell on the positives of our circumstances in a shameless attempt at brainwashing myself and everyone around me. The joy of hiking, for example, is considerably diminished now that the hunting season is well and truly underway, for it is truly difficult to allow one's mind to fully run free while the echoing sound of gunshots sporadically pierce the air, an all too concrete testimony to the fact that both rural hunters and wild boar (wild boar!) are prowling the surrounding hills. Might I one day prove to be the victim, *Deliverance*-like, of a determined local who has been anxiously surveying my daily rituals with suspicion, resolved to preserve the purity of his countryside? Such flights of fancy no longer seem quite so paranoid once one learns that one is being watched...

And then it must be admitted that the weather is not always perfect. In itself this is all perfectly reasonable, of course, and it can certainly be great fun to hunker down and watch a swirling thunderstorm flash angrily across the valley secure in the knowledge that, as renters, the rising water in the basement is not particularly our concern. But a few consecutive days of inclement weather do have the disturbing effect of distinctly reinforcing how weather-dependent one is in these surroundings, how alarmingly important a regular dose of sunshine has become to one's suddenly precarious mental health—how much, in short, like an animal one has become.

You protest that cities are expensive. And so they are. But I know why: Because they often contain people who move there of their own free will! Because one might occasionally run into some lively souls there who have finished high school or have even gone to (gasp!) university! Because the exterior weather conditions do not strictly determine the scope of one's activities in a locale where numerous stimulating indoor options exist that don't involve playing "spin the bottle" with one's immediate family relatives! Because one might unhesitatingly assume that within the safe confines of a sophisticated urban area, one's children might receive a level of education greater than that of your average migrant farm worker!

Enough.

I am here in the Midi working on my French like a Lycée student developing his Latin: reading texts and doing grammatical exercises, while patently unable to speak with any genuine ability or coherence. Unable or unwilling? Perhaps both. Here in the wilds of Languedoc, where the prospect of social interaction is limited to nodding bonjour to knuckle-dragging neighbours or haltingly responding to babbling tele-solicitors, it's truly hard to work up an appetite for discussion in any language. I'm starting to reach the not entirely unobvious conclusion that if I'm going to be living in France, I might as well be *living in France*. Not bad after 2 months, isn't it? Imagine the profundities that I might discover by Christmas at this rate?

Last weekend, in a desperate move to extricate ourselves from the mind-numbing provincialism of our immediate environs, we took advantage of A's repeated entreaties to head over to Provence and visit him in Cassis, dropping by Aix-en-Provence for good measure to take a look around.

Cassis was, of course, physically stunning with the imposing *Cap Canaille* dwarfing the pretty harbour lined with charming cafés, and the fjord-like *calanques* are most impressive.

It was all most beautiful, but still and all somehow *unreal*— with Cassis undeniably spectacular but still definitely missing the vitality of the genuine. Aix was considerably more substantial, if obviously less physically impressive, but still somehow, intangibly, artificial, a bit like living in a toy store, I would imagine. A fantastic place for a sabbatical, I have not the slightest doubt, but to really live? I don't really think so. Of course, there is no comparison to our present surroundings: I'd take the plastic post-card-like environs of Cassis over the mindless earthiness of Le Pouget any day of the week, but that is hardly the point: if the goal is to drastically curtail the frequency of our future *déménagements*, it doesn't make a great deal of sense to compare prospective surroundings with Le Pouget, but rather to the sort of place we could happily see ourselves settling down in for the foreseeable future.

Still, it was wonderful to get out and see other places, particularly those by the sea. We decided, on an impulse and thanks to the ever-gracious A, to return there for a week's worth of further explorations during next week's *Toussaint* holiday (the notion of a fall school break, it should be admitted to give your countrymen their fair due, being the single most impressive aspect of the French public educational system we have discovered to date), before heading up to Lyon the following weekend.

Although it's a bit of a stretch to maintain that Irena and

I have done anything to particularly merit a holiday, it is unquestionably true that the kids have by enduring the first two months of school here, so off we go—lucky for us we're travelling with them).

As far as our brief sojourn to Lyon goes, please don't get angry at the thought of us going off to your fair city without informing you, family members and so forth—needless to say, we certainly are not trying to cause any offense, but we just thought it would be best to quietly get a sense of the place before even considering more "serious" investigations about possible relocation.

Another locale we recognize we need to investigate more fully is Montpellier—which should be, of course, a good deal easier given its proximity. As you know, it has so far produced rather a mixed response from us that has, overall, not been tremendously inspiring, but we well recognize that we certainly haven't explored matters there terribly rigorously so far and are resolved to do what we can to redress matters on that front on our return.

And there is this, the potential trump card: they seem to have a real baseball facility in Montpellier for Louis. The kid has definitely earned that from his recent travails (yes, yet another English word *masquerading* as a French one). And yes, sure, me too, I suppose: have I mentioned that the only things I miss about North America are baseball and (ready access to) New York City? Well, it's true. At this point an offer of a front office (Back office? Third base?) job from the New York Yankees would have me immediately scurrying back across the pond. Feel free to pass the message along to Mr Steinbrenner, should you come across him in your travels. Even the Mets would be fine—beggars can't be choosers.

Speaking of sports, in a fervent desire to adapt as quickly as possible to our surroundings, we have also tried to immerse ourselves in the local sports scene here, unfortunately with only limited success. The kids are big soccer fans, as you know, so that is a good start, but the truth is that we are all deeply out of touch with the teams and personalities over here. It is, I don't mind admitting, awfully difficult just understanding all the myriad structural details between local leagues, national leagues, European champion's leagues, Euro 2008 qualifying events, World Cup qualifying events and so forth.

Louis appears to be miles ahead of the rest of us and has even adopted Lyon as his favourite French soccer team, doubtless in a concrete move to distance himself from his classmates who are all fervent Marseille supporters (although the fact that Lyon is regularly perched atop the standings might also have something to do with it), but that is pretty well as far as it goes. Soccer is not the easiest game for me to watch on television, I have to admit, but verges on the impossible if I can't somehow find a team to passionately align myself with (or against). I *did* manage to sit through an entire game between Lens and Monaco the other day, I'm proud to tell you, by resolutely rooting against Monaco (spoiled, snooty, monarchical, superficial Rivierans!), but such opportunities to firmly engage are, so far, fairly rare. Must try harder.

But by far the biggest sporting news around these parts of

late is France's hosting of the Rugby World Cup. Rugby, I was surprised to discover, is actually quite popular in France, particularly in the south-west, where, as our Michelin Green Guide euphemistically says, "it strikes a particular chord with the robust Occitan temperament". Indeed. Rather like, I would imagine, feeding Christians to the lions struck a particular chord with the robust Roman temperament.

At any rate, in a determined effort to get in tune with the surrounding *zeitgeist*, Louis and I spent a couple of confused evenings peering helplessly at Rugby World Cup games on television, desperately trying to figure out what the hell was going on; and, aside from the most rudimentary and obvious conclusions (e.g. this is not a game for anyone who is not convulsed with homoerotic desire—not that there's anything wrong with that, of course), failing rather spectacularly. France beat New Zealand by the way, which we gathered was an upset of nothing less than biblical proportions that gave rise to an overpowering display of cock-a-hooping that was abruptly quelched when *Les Bleus* lost to the dreaded English in the semi-finals the following week. So that's the sports news for the moment.

Meanwhile, Irena continues her weekly exchanges with "The Cheese Man" whom she is now convinced would make an ideal chess partner for me given his locally unique combination of clear elocution and reading ability (she recently witnessed him idly flipping through a magazine while waiting for customers) and is tempted to ask him if he plays the game, but is somewhat concerned that in doing so she will inadvertently stumble onto some typically colourful

French turn of phrase whereby a woman asking a man if he might be inclined to play chess with her husband is really investigating his interest and availability in participating in a *ménage à quatre* with herself, a goat and a rooster. Needless to say, any advice on this front would be appreciated...

We sincerely hope that all is well with all of you and that your kids are merrily gearing up for an enjoyable Hallowe'en experience. Speaking of which, Hallowe'en, quite surprisingly, seems to be something that people actually care about over here—we had always thought it was strictly a North American extravaganza. Is this a recent phenomenon caused by globalization/the American Hyper-U/Toys-R-Us hegemony or have the French long given the pagans their fair due? Do tell. Needless to say, we'd ask some *Pougétois* for their views, but they're all far too scaaaaaaaaaaaaaaaaaaaaaaaaaaary for us.

Fearfully yours,

Howard

A Decision

November 4, 2007

Dear N & L,

Greetings again my dear Lyonnais amis. We have just returned from our little Toussaint break—a week back in Cassis (via Nîmes, the Camargue and Marseille) followed by this past weekend in your home stomping ground of Lugdunum.

Cassis was charming, warm, visually stunning and plastic as ever with ample opportunity to relax with the kids outside of our now-normal milieu of grubby, rough and tumble *vendangeurs* and stifling parochialism. We filled our days by hiking along the calanques, swimming in the azure waters of the Mediterranean or just lolling around A's apartment playing games (he characteristically insisted we stay there while he went elsewhere—it seemed impolite to ask where, exactly—visions of cuckolded Cassisists brandishing shotguns were definitely dancing in my head, however).

We went up to Aix a few times to check out a few uninspiring "international schools", sample its relaxed, sabbatical friendly charm by strolling along the welcoming boulevards and even managed to procure a sushi lunch (thereby satisfying a strong, pent-up demand for Asian food that is yet another unexpected byproduct of Le Pouget monotony). Ever the culturally sensitive (not to mention culturally deprived) tourists, we also made sure to check out Aix's decidedly unimpressive museums and galleries (in case you are ever tempted to trek up to the *Cézanne Atelier*, by the way, don't bother—one could get considerably more inspiration and appreciation for the artistic lifestyle by downloading Simon Schama videos at one's local Starbucks).

Given that Aix seems to be universally regarded around those parts as the sophisticated sister of gritty Marseille, this doesn't bode terribly well for the desirability of *la cité phocéenne*—which, from our very brief drive-by experience, certainly struck us as quite lively, in a decidedly *French Connection* sort of way, but still and all probably not the most suitable place to settle down with two children whom one actually loves.

The Camargue, meanwhile, was filled with mud, bulls, horses, flamingos and tourists, as expected—an interesting experience well worth seeing once, but one that your intrepid traveller quickly finds leaving him quite *saturé*, as our friends at *France Telecom* would say. We even stopped by the aptly-named Aigues-Mortes on our way towards the Camargue to get the full tourist experience, dutifully spending an hour or two walking around the perfectly-preserved ramparts of the city, gazing at the satellite dishes below and idly wondering why so many people were so keen to still establish their abode in a walled village on swampland where it was impossible to even see a sunset. Suffice it to say the experience gave us a renewed sense of appreciation for the relative intellectual acuity of *Les Pougétois*—as Feynman so famously said, "There's always room at the bottom."

In short, it was all an interesting and enjoyable break from our somewhat lugubrious routine of guilt and self-flagellation at the prospect of regularly subjecting our children to the inanities of "the educational experience" of Languedoc, but still and all hardly the sort of thing that is itself enormously captivating or intrinsically beguiling. To us at least, virtually everywhere in "the South" seems plagued with people—both locals and tourists—far more desirous of ripping off their shirts and getting a tan than indulging in any sort of intellectual stimulation whatsoever (speaking of which—why is it that so many significantly overweight men feel that they are entitled to thrust their naked bellies into full public view at the slightest provocation? There really should be laws against that sort of thing).

And as the week elapsed and Irena and I began to morosely indulge in yet another round of "where on earth should we go?" I couldn't help shaking the growing drumbeat of despair that was shouting "WHAT THE HELL ARE YOU DOING HERE? WHY DON'T YOU JUST ADMIT THAT THE ENTIRE FRENCH FORAY WAS A DISASTER AND JUST MOVE TO CALIFORNIA?!"

And then we reached Lyon.

So it's difficult to know how to say this without sounding churlish. Perhaps it's better to begin with a few disclaimers in the hopes of minimizing any future misunderstandings.

I well realize that, given the rather abrupt nature of our departure, there wasn't a great deal of opportunity for studied, measured reflection or contemplation of next steps.

Relatedly, our personal relationship at the time, hitherto encumbered by the impediment of the professional, might not have been nearly as open as it has subsequently become, making it considerably more difficult at the time to have an honest and candid dialogue on our future life trajectory.

My overwhelming feelings of disgust, disdain and disinterest at having anything further to do with my fellow *Homo sapiens* for the indefinite future did rather prejudice my ability to take a realistic look at things, particularly with respect to establishing an appropriate environment for my children and other real issues that I would soon find myself faced with.

I know well that it is often difficult to be truly objective about one's home town. Whenever anybody comes to Toronto, for example, I seem to spend the vast majority of my time in a vain attempt to squelch their enthusiasm for things that I find to be largely superficial and uninteresting.

And yet.

Our expectations were high, it must be said—dangerously so, we repeatedly told ourselves. In a world where the only consistent factor suddenly seemed to be a palpable difference between our rapidly lowering standards and reality, we still found it impossible to approach our encounter with Lyon with anything other than unbridled optimism—after all, the *real France* must surely be somewhere else in the country other than the luminous yet potentially unaffordable capital? Such hopeful sentiments, we told ourselves, with a grim sense of foreboding, must surely be a recipe for disaster as yet another bubble would burst and, in addition to our own sense of disappointment, we would also be faced with the unpalatable task of having to relay such sentiments to the two of you. So as we sailed northward up the *Route du Soleil* with the skies suddenly turning a bleak and frigid grey from the piercing Mediterranean blue, our adumbrations seemed sadly, once again, right on the mark.

I'm not sure what I had been expecting, probably something like a smaller version of Paris—attractive surely, in its own way, but somehow still both vaguely provincial yet unlivable. In short likely ***good enough,*** all things considered, and unquestionably a damned sight better than anything we have around us now, but still and all hardly an ideal destination in itself. Capital of French gastronomy and all that—well, fine. But then, I am hardly a foodie, and anyway such things are hardly a top priority for us given our current lifestyle and concerns.

We settled into our non-descript and vaguely unimpressive Euro-hotel and strolled towards the centre of town, moving briskly through the cool weather. I am telling you all these uninspiring details lest you think that we were blinded by uncharacteristically positive events. We were not. The hotel was little more than adequate, while the weather (until Monday, which was a beautiful, crisp fall day) was basically crappy.

And yet, none of that mattered in the slightest. For the first time since we set foot in France, we felt unequivocal enthusiasm about a place. None of this "Well, if you take away this and that, it wouldn't be bad" or "Parts of it are quite nice" or the still more defeatist Canadianesque "Everyone has to live somewhere", but simply: "Yes! Now *that's* more like it!"

Of course, we can't claim to have gotten anything more than just a tiny flavour of things, but that flavour was most enticing and—better still—the more we saw, the more we liked. The core is attractive, of course, and elegant, but the pace of life seems somehow slightly less officiously hectic and mindlessly busy, intangibly more enjoyable than in a larger city like Paris or London. The Roman ruins are impressive, but even more so is the adjacent Gallo-Romaine museum with its splendid displays and perfectly contoured setting that fits so harmoniously and unobtrusively with the landscape. The Museé des Beaux Arts is, of course, no Louvre—to put it extremely mildly—but we still managed to spend a most enjoyable visit there on our first afternoon without even getting to the second floor. Even the Miniature Museum, which Irena and I had resigned ourselves to submitting to for the sake of the children, turned out to be well worth the visit and considerably beyond its tourist trap-esque exterior.

Future investigations proved ever more revealing. **Alfred Brendel**, it seems, is making one of his few public performances in 2008 in Lyon (King Alfred! We pinched ourselves—the news was as close as this atheist has ever come to feeling that he has received a divine sign), as is the sparkling **Martha Argerich** in a few weeks' time. This is impressive stuff by *New York City* standards, let alone our present cultural environment where a day at the beach inevitably involves watching children hurl mud at each other. And the hits just kept on coming: the Parc de la Tête d'Or was nothing less than a shock. Finally, evidence that the French had taken the obvious step of putting a beautiful, expansive park in the middle of the city. The morning of our departure we spent driving around various neighbourhoods, stopping here and there to check out several international schools that we had researched on the internet beforehand. More sighs of relief as the schools appeared to be, finally, gratifyingly solid and professional-looking—for once we seemed firmly in the land where ambitious websites might conceivably correspond to reality.

The whole thing had the undeniable tinge of feeling like we were waking up from a rather bizarre dream that had gone on far too long. I would be lying if I didn't admit that by the time we were leaving, in the great spirit of transference and scape-goating that the human condition is so obviously prone to, both Irena and I began to feel increasingly nonplussed at the two of you, wondering how it was even remotely ***possible*** that you did not ***INSIST*** that we ***immediately*** relocate to your home town instead of allowing us to subject ourselves to the indignities and absurdities of Le Pouget and surrounding environs. A clever plot to destroy any illusions we might have of French rural life, thereby ensuring we would fully appreciate big-city living when the time (quickly) came? A selfish determination to be exposed to rural anecdotes? A subconscious desire to punish us for leaving the two of you mired in provincial Ontario as we cavalierly trekked off to sample *la dolce vita à la française*? Vindictiveness, bitterness or pettiness I can at least understand...

Anyway, it is an enormous relief to finally convey that things have become much clearer. Our French wave function, to use a physics metaphor, has finally collapsed. Enough looking around. Enough compromise. Enough talking. We have a new slogan around here as of yesterday: Lyon or California. Enough.

The only thing uncertain at this point is the timing. Moving over Christmas would be naturally ideal for us under the right circumstances, but might well not be feasible given the fact that we are already in November and there is much to sort out. The international schools in Lyon don't generally appear to be terribly enthusiastic at the prospect of taking students mid-year: it seems they are actually (Hooray!) motivated by a desire to create a maximally-appropriate learning environment for their students and are somewhat fearful that this could be jeopardized by substantial inflows of new students at irregular times. They also (Hooray again!) appear to have entrance exams of a sort, which naturally makes it difficult for us to ascertain precisely when (or indeed if) our kids can get accepted there (or, more worryingly, if both of them can get into the same school).

There is, of course, the not entirely negligible or automatic matter of finding appropriate temporary accommodation in Lyon, giving notice here and all of that. Under the circumstances, depending on the responses from the respective schools, we may well wind up sticking it out in Le Pouget a while longer, home-schooling one or both of the kids if need be and supplementing our efforts with private French lessons somewhere, likely Montpellier. On the other hand, it is indeed possible that we might get lucky and find a way to leave earlier somehow. Either way, however, it is an indescribable relief to finally have a clear sense of direction, to have found a place that we are truly excited about going to. In short, after months of lolling around aimlessly, we suddenly find ourselves faced with the prospect of another series of pressure-filled, life-changing decisions.

Thank goodness, I say. Bring on the police sirens and the traffic jams; give me entrance exams, apartment leases and stress. Any more relaxing in the country might just kill me.

Urbanophilically yours,

Howard

The End of the Affair

November 11, 2007

Dear N & L,

Thanks very much for your recent phone call and heartfelt encouragement in our quest to move sooner rather than later to your home stomping ground. While it is still too early to be saying anything with absolute certainty, it is beginning to look increasingly like we might actually be able to put country living behind us by New Year's. We're busily preparing the kids' *dossiers* as we speak, but the kindly yet sophisticated folk at the still-impressive Lyon international school seem determined to do their utmost to assist us in making our escape back to civilization. I think, quite frankly, they are taking pity on us, overwhelmed by the uniqueness of our situation—my guess is that we are the only foreign nationals who have ever arrived on their doorstep via Languedoc. Fingers crossed: once we know that the kids are in, we will hastily look for some temporary flat to hang our collective hats, and with any luck at all we might be able to have the whole business settled by early December.

Given all of this, we find that we have naturally slipped into a different perspective, already regarding Le Pouget from a far-away, nostalgic light as our French Ellis Island, a springboard to bigger and brighter things, rather than the purgatory that it had so often seemed, in real time, to be.

Meanwhile, we are resolutely exploring the surrounding region with a new passion, aware as we now are that we will soon be located in an altogether different setting. So it was that we have just returned from an excursion to Nîmes and the famed Pont du Gard, where we spent the day duly appreciating the Roman engineering brilliance of constructing remarkably long-lasting structures to both transport water and amuse the rabble with gory spectacles. Such visible evidence of so much history certainly does give one a different perspective on things, provoking stray ruminations on the true meaning of "culture". Perhaps in 2000 years, I found myself musing, responsible North American parents will diligently take their children on Sunday excursions to iPod museums or the ruins of the Air Canada Centre.

Or perhaps not.

I am pleased to report that, as we move steadily towards our shining Lyonnais future, the kids are noticeably starting to relax, increasingly secure in the expectation that their academic endeavours here are finally drawing to a close.

The other day, Louis' English teacher asked him to present the class with a set of uniquely Canadian idioms for their collective edification. After scratching his head for a while to come up with an appropriate expression (I can't think of any myself), he naturally decided that it would be ever so much more reasonable, not to mention enjoyable, to simply invent some instead; and he has thrust himself into this literary task with customary gusto ("Get that hockey stick out of your ear!" "Like a snowstorm in July!").

As the supposedly responsible ones in the family, we probably should have at least pretended to dissuade him from such fraudulent activity, but our still-lingering resentment towards this absurd woman who coldly informed our son that he didn't speak English with the correct accent combined with the sheer delight at the prospect of being responsible for generations of Languedociens invoking mythical Canadian metaphors was simply too good an opportunity to pass up. We joined in emphatically ("A loony for your thoughts!" "As flaky as a Vancouverite!").

Emmy, meanwhile, unbeknownst to us, has quietly asserted herself as a star rugby player during the regular weekly training session in gym class. It took us some time to catch on to what was happening, given her constant outward protestations of how ridiculous the game was, but recently Irena and I decided to spy on her (the training sessions occur on the public soccer field across from her school behind the *Mairie*) and discovered, much to our amusement, that she has become nothing less than the class rugby terror, charging this way and that to score try after try. Moreover, this was, I must relate, no watered-down game of "touch rugby" as I had been naively expecting, but the real full contact experience, with children hurling themselves at their compatriots with gay abandon.

You ask, enviously no doubt, about the weather. The temperature has cooled off considerably, largely owing to the brisk winds that come periodically whistling through the valley. There is still a luscious abundance of sunlight, however, and the heat of the afternoon sun can often be quite significant, forcing one to oscillate awkwardly between sunlight and shade like some Goldilocks-like search for an appropriate comfort zone. Well, things are tough all over, of course. Has the snow started there yet?

As it happens, the strength of the Mediterranean sun is actually quite perplexing to me. The relatively warm temperatures around these parts can presumably be accounted for by a combination of the Mediterranean, surrounding geography, Gulf stream and so forth, but I really can't figure out why the sun is so piercingly strong here, given that Le Pouget is actually at roughly the same latitude as Toronto. I've asked a few physicist friends of mine about this when we chatted on the phone and they seem equally miffed—further proof (if any more were needed) that the vast majority of scientists are unable to say anything useful about any issue of genuine relevance whatsoever. Do let me know if you have any light to bear, as it were, on the subject: perhaps I'll do a google search on it the next time I bother to pass by an "internet café". But I'll probably forget.

Le Pouget, meanwhile, merrily continues marching steadily along its own rhythms, oblivious to such abstruse concerns. The surrounding vineyards are being drastically pruned right down to their stumps as the great dormant season seems set to begin. The pace of life, never fast, seems to have moved a notch or two lower still.

But that is mere appearance—the view of the unsophisticated eye—for what a remarkable week of truly unexpected developments your intrepid correspondents have experienced!

The first sign of unusualness was when we noticed the neighbourhood electrician taking time out from his months of vigilant archway-standing to instead sit down and work on a sketch of the village square (which is not actually square, as it happens, but never mind). An artistic electrician! How positively, archetypically (as it were) quaint!

Our excitement at this discovery—so much in keeping with our romantic sense of village life that was so methodically shattered over the past three months—was unavoidably tinged with a sigh of regret as well as a flitter of paranoia: could it be that the *Pougétois* were all simply pretending to be as monumentally uninteresting as they appeared, resolutely sticking it out until the unobliging tourists had finally resolved to pack it in and leave town before they promptly brought out their easels and chess tables?

Then came the latest installment from Irena's affair (I use the word in its social sense, *bien sûr*) with the famous Cheese Man. This Friday's episode has amazingly revealed that *Monsieur Fromage* hails from (wait for it)....Paris! ("I knew it!" exclaimed Irena, striding into the house with her baguettes and bag of cheese. "I *knew* he couldn't be from around here!")

Apparently he made his escape from the Northern drizzle only quite recently, and he too hardly finds himself well integrated in the local scene. "I can't understand what they're saying most of the time" he apparently confessed to Irena, flicking a thumb towards the other market merchants. "You don't want to stay here too long or you might wind up talking like them."

This increasing resonance between ourselves and the Cheese

Man was mildly unsettling for Yours Truly, who is slowly beginning to appreciate that the Parisian *Fromager* might represent more serious competition than I had first assumed—all the more reason to leave here sooner rather than later. But still and all this news pales in comparison to what follows.

On returning from our weekly trek to the nearby internet outlet, Irena casually informed me that she had recognized one of the nearby customers as a *Pougétois* parent at the village school and was about to go over to greet her when she noticed that the lady in question was fully immersed in a porn site.

"Well, whatever," I declared airily, determined to demonstrate my tolerance, "It's not my place to be commenting on how other people spend their time."

"No, you don't understand", responded Irena. "She wasn't just ***looking*** at the site. She was ***developing*** the site." Indeed, it seems that the aforementioned parent was very much the star of the show.

Notwithstanding my previous professions of open-mindedness, this **did** seem rather a different state of affairs—at the very least I was determined to pay more attention to my environs next time I went somewhere to check my email.

Could Le Pouget be somehow the centre of a bourgeoning pornographic film industry? Might this be a more plausible explanation for the mysterious dearth of local high-speed internet connection (when even a *star **and** director/producer* has to use public facilities to develop her product!) than the creation of the new *Médiatheque*? Moreover, perhaps this new *Médiatheque* is itself really nothing more than a production and distribution centre for a covert local industry. Could this somehow explain the consistently friendly demeanour of the locals? Their corresponding lack of interest in chess? We simply don't know; and time is, sadly, running out on our attempt to unravel the increasingly layered local mysteries.

Perhaps I should have explicitly inquired with the neighbours, for I had a golden opportunity several days later when Richard, quite clearly inebriated beyond repair, knocked aggressively on the door shortly after 7 pm on a Saturday night.

"I hope the roosters aren't making too much noise for you!" he slurred his crazy, cryptic code, as he glanced up at me in evident determination to enter our home.

"Not at all", I replied quickly, sweeping stray copies of *Le Figaro* off the table as I waved him to a nearby chair while desperately trying to ascertain what the hell he wanted from me. I hadn't spoken more than three words to him since the ill-fated "make-up dinner" of months back.

An hour later, after a painfully polite and completely disjointed conversation about nothing whatsoever, I suddenly understood what was happening: Béatrice must have kicked him out the house for a while, or perhaps he had simply misplaced his key in a drunken stupor. Either way, he was clearly at wit's end (admittedly, I can't help cattily emphasizing, not a terribly long journey) and had, out of sheer desperation, resolved to give the foreign fascists one final try to assist him in his hour of need. Sensing what might be my last opportunity to unequivocally redeem myself as both a good neighbour and a sensitive soul firmly imbued with the requisite French spirit of *fraternité*, I sucked in my gut, made several carafes of coffee and chatted mindlessly with him for ***three solid hours***—much to the sheer horror, I might add, of my wife and children, who had quickly retired upstairs to the furthest corner of the house to play card games.

I am delighted to report to you that I made it through the entire escapade with my sensitivity credentials (such as they are) firmly intact, playing the unimpeachably perfect host throughout. And when I finally closed the door behind him, after having warmly accepted his kind invitation to come over to his place on some future occasion to sample his special recipe for procuring sparkling wine from goat's milk, I felt suffused with pride at both my stamina and my rapidly developing social skills that had, I was certain, erased all of my earlier *faux pas*.

But I never did ask him about the Le Pouget porn ring - that probably would have been too much. And with any luck at all, I'll be out of here before I get another chance.

Anxiously yours,

Howard

Postscript

We did, indeed, move to Lyon in the beginning of 2008, resettling in a neighbouring village (on the outskirts!) a few years later.

Despite the shambolic nature of our thoroughly ill-prepared flight into the Languedoc wilderness, we never did return permanently to Canada. Nor, of course, did we return to Languedoc for any longer than a day or two. But the place still holds a very strong place in our hearts, with many surprisingly vivid memories. It was a clear point of demarcation for all of us: the beginning of a new stage in our lives.

Our children attended Lyon's Cité Scolaire Internationale right through to their baccalauréat, which did, indeed, give them the opportunity to have a good-quality bilingual education—particularly, it must be admitted, from the French teachers, who were typically leagues ahead of their English colleagues.

On the political side of things, we've witnessed how the enthusiasm for Nicolas Sarkozy's presidency rapidly turned to disdain for his "hyperactive style", paving the way for the election of François Hollande five years later, who successfully ran on the platform of not being Nicolas Sarkozy (i.e. *l'homme normal*)—a role he was eminently qualified for.

After the brief post-election euphoria, the French quickly turned on Hollande too, suddenly appreciating that not being Nicolas Sarkozy was hardly, in itself, the stuff that impressive presidents are made of, summarily labelling him as "ineffectual".

The deeply unpopular Hollande was duly replaced five years later by Emmanuel Macron (capitalizing on an unexpected scandal which sidelined the seeming heir apparent in the usual left-right shuffle, François Fillon) who, far from portraying himself as *un homme normal*, was determined to demonstrate that he was a man of ideas and action. His victory, all too characteristically, was met with unbridled optimism for the requisite half-hour or so before people began to suspect that, as a man of ideas and action he was actually intent on doing things, whereupon he was inevitably deemed "monarchical" and consequently suffered a similar plunge in popularity.

And so it goes.

As the years rolled by, all of that became increasingly irrelevant to us. We noticed it, of course—how could you not?—but it never really seemed worth paying all that much attention to. This was France, after all—whoever was in charge there was a similar sort of cycle to things: reforms would be announced, people would loudly protest, more talks would be had, the protesters would become emboldened, compromises would be declared, more emboldened protesters, and eventually everything would return to the status quo.

Best to meet the whole business with a Gallic shrug.

But while I almost never get worked up about the particulars, and I am usually quite unsympathetic to the issues of the moment (I have frequently had, for example, a strong urge to ship planeloads of whining French university students to America to let them glimpse firsthand what it's like to live in a world of non-subsidized higher education—and don't even get me started with the "gilets jaunes"), there is a certain, intangible resonance that I share with people here: for all of their hypocrisy and selfishness and general silliness (and there is much of all three here, of course, as there is everywhere), there is a core understanding that all of these societal structures and associated *big topics*—capitalism, politics, government, and all the rest—simply exist in order to enable human flourishing. The French almost always get the details wrong, in my view. But they invariably get the big picture right.

And the big picture matters. Whenever I find myself in the Anglosphere—the differences between English-speaking countries seem to be shrinking at an alarming rate and it makes less and less sense to bother to distinguish between them, in my opinion—I increasingly sense that the big picture is being rather decidedly missed. I can't help feeling that in some very basic way a real problem that pervades all of those societies is that, on the whole, people don't seem to appreciate that they are going to die. And so they do not, on the whole, genuinely focus on living.

This might seem maudlin, I appreciate—and deeply out of context with the rest of this little book. Well, perhaps. But that's what you get when you spend all this time writing social commentary: preachiness becomes an occupational hazard, I'm afraid.

I'm often asked by my Canadian friends if, after all this time in France, I "feel French"—some even ask if I have "become French". Well, no. That sentiment—while perfectly understandable, I realize, in a Canadian context—simply makes no sense here. I will never "be French" any more than I will be an 18th-century Ottoman Sultan or an ancient Greek merchant or Roger Federer. It's not about pretending to be something you're not. It's about finding the place where you can best become what you want to be.

There is an image I have these days when I reflect upon what I love about this place, why I feel so comfortable here. I think about Jean Le Cam, the *Vendée Globe* sailor who spent 80 days at sea (saving someone's life along the way), finally coming off his boat and ignoring the barrage of questions from reporters as he stood on the dock doing a little dance, swaying to the music in his head.

Le Cam has not, clearly, had an easy life. He is not a wealthy man. He wound up finishing 4th in the race. But to my mind he is a real winner.

www.ingramcontent.com/pod-product-compliance
Lightning Source LLC
Chambersburg PA
CBHW030910080526
44589CB00010B/232